THE
BABY BOOMER
TRIVIA BOOK

TAKE A FUN WALK DOWN MEMORY LANE WITH THE 1950S, 1960S, 1970S AND 1980S TRIVIA AND QUIZZES

CHARLIE MILLER

ISBN: 978-1-64845-124-9

CONTENTS

INTRODUCTION

Can you remember the Moon landings of 1969? If so, can you answer this: What was the name of the *Apollo 11* astronaut who remained behind in the lunar module, while Neil Armstrong and Buzz Aldrin explored the Moon's surface?

Perhaps the 1970s was more your era? In which case, can you remember what the first horror movie in cinema history to be nominated for a Best Picture Oscar was? Here is a clue - it came out in 1973…

Or what about the 1980s? Is that a period of time that is fresher in your memory? In which case, do you know what city played host to the famous Miracle on Ice in 1980? And for that matter, can you name the larger sporting event of which the game was just one small part?

If questions like these have you racking your brain - or even better, bursting to shout out the correct answer - then this is very much the book for you! This is *The Baby Boomer Trivia Book*.

What follows here are four decades' worth of quiz questions, memories, and random trivia, covering the

Baby Boomer era - which is, all the years from the 1950s to the 1980s.

Inside each decade's section of the book, you will find yourself pitted against 50 fiendish history and pop culture questions, covering everything from the news and current affairs of the time to topics like sports, music, and television.

And along the way, there are plenty of random facts and trivia lists to keep you entertained (and to give your brain a short break!) between rounds.

So, let's make a start!

We are heading back the furthest in time down memory lane for our first quiz here, starting way back in the 1950s... (Oh, and as for the questions above? The answers you are after are Michael Collins, *The Exorcist*, Lake Placid, and the Winter Olympics!)

PART 1:

THE 1950s

IN THE NEWS

THE 1950s

1. Which of these famous figures of the 1950s served as Wisconsin Senator from 1947 to 1957?
   a. Harry Truman
   b. Joseph McCarthy
   c. Douglas MacArthur
   d. Lyndon Johnson

2. In 1951, President Truman delivered the very first transcontinental television broadcast in US history. Where was he at the time?
   a. New York
   b. San Francisco
   c. Houston
   d. Anchorage

3. President Eisenhower won the presidential election in the same year that which of these other global leaders ascended to power?
   a. Queen Elizabeth II
   b. Charles de Gaulle
   c. Winston Churchill
   d. Leonid Brezhnev

4. *Castle Bravo* made the headlines in 1953. What was it?
   a. Atomic bomb
   b. Doomsday cult
   c. Naval battleship
   d. Space shuttle

5. Which of these mountains was summited for the first time in 1953?
   a. Mount Blanc
   b. Mount Everest
   c. Mount McKinley
   d. True or False? NASA was founded in the 1950s.

6. Which famous artist died in a car crash in New York in 1956?

a. Andy Warhol
b. Henry Matisse
c. Edward Hopper
d. Jackson Pollock

7. In which of these fields did Jonas Salk become a famous name in the 1950s?

    a. Art
    b. Astronomy
    c. Politics
    d. Medicine

8. In 1954, what was the chief concern of President Eisenhower's so-called "domino theory"?

    a. War in outer space
    b. Economic recession
    c. Spread of Communism
    d. Education standards

9. In what year did Alaska and Hawaii become the 49th and 50th US states?

    a. 1951
    b. 1954
    c. 1957
    d. 1959

ANSWERS

1. B. Joseph McCarthy. It was during his tenure as Senator from Wisconsin that McCarthy's crusade against Communist infiltration began, and the term "McCarthyism" was coined three years later in 1950.

2. B. San Francisco. Truman had previously delivered the very first live televised State of the Union Address in January 1947 and made history again four years later when, on September 4, 1951 (at 7.30 p.m. Pacific Time) he gave the principal speech at the Japanese Peace Treaty Conference in San Francisco. For the first time in political history, viewers on both sides of the country could watch the broadcast live.

3. A. Queen Elizabeth II. Eisenhower roundly defeated his Democrat opponent Adlai Stephenson in the November 1952 election - taking the electoral college by 442 to 89 - and took to the presidency early the following year. Across the Atlantic, Britain's longest reigning monarch also rose to power in 1952, on the death of her father George VI, and was officially crowned at her coronation in London the following spring.

4. A. Atomic bomb. Detonated in the Marshall Islands' remote Bikini Atoll as part of the ongoing Operation Castle atomic program, Castle Bravo remains the most powerful weapon ever used by the United States.

5. B. Mount Everest. New Zealand mountaineer Edmund Hillary and Nepalese Sherpa Tenzing Norgay made the first successful (and first documented) ascent of Everest on May 29, 1953. Two decades earlier, explorers George Mallory and Andrew Irvine made the same attempt but never returned, and it remains unclear whether or not they reached the peak before their disappearance.

6. True! It might have been a decade before the Moon landings, but NASA was founded as the space race ramped up in 1958.

7. D. Jackson Pollock. Pollock was just 44 years old at the time of his tragic death.

8. D. Medicine. Salk developed the first functioning polio vaccine, based on an inactive poliomyelitis virus, and demonstrated it in 1955. As the vaccine was rolled out worldwide, its effectiveness quickly proved obvious: cases of polio around the world fell by over 10,000%, to barely 30 cases per year in the 2000s.

9. C. Spread of Communism. Eisenhower believed that if Communism were to prove successful in just one Southeast Asian nation, the entire region would fall like dominoes, one country at a time.

10. D. 1959. The Territory of Alaska was officially admitted to the Union on January 3, 1959, followed a little under eight months later by Hawaii on August 21.

DID YOU KNOW?

- The 1950s saw author Ernest Hemingway become only one of seven authors in history to have won both a Pulitzer Prize and a Nobel Prize for Literature - and, even more impressively, he won them back-to-back in 1953 and 1954!

- The US population was around half what it is today in the 1950s. According to census data, the US was home to 157.8 million people in 1950.

- In 1955, President Eisenhower signed legislation that henceforth legally required the words "In God We Trust" to appear on all United States currency.

- The 1950s saw some bizarre weather records: in 1955, one foot of hail fell in Rushmore, Minnesota.

- Coca-Cola was sold in cans for the first time in the 1950s. Before then, it had only ever been sold in glass bottles!

MOVIES & TV

THE 1950s

1. Which American actress was nominated for a record six Best Supporting Actress Oscars in her lifetime — five of which were for a string of movies in the 1950s - but never won?

   a. Angela Lansbury
   b. Thelma Ritter
   c. Celeste Holm
   d. Gloria Graeme

2. What former radio comedy serial made the leap to television in 1954 and eventually ran for more than 200 episodes?
   a. Bewitched
   b. I Dream of Jeannie
   c. Father Knows Best
   d. The Larkins

3. Legendary director Alfred Hitchcock had a string of hits in the 1950s - but which of these was from the 1960s, not the 50s?
   a. Rear Window
   b. Psycho
   c. Vertigo
   d. North by Northwest

4. Who was James Stewart's somewhat co-star in 1956's *The Man Who Knew Too Much?*
   a. Lucille Ball
   a. Marilyn Monroe
   b. Doris Day
   c. Marlene Dietrich

5. Who became the first Black actor to receive an Academy Award nomination for Best Actor for his role in the 1958 film *The Defiant Ones?*
   a. Rupert Crosse
   b. Sidney Poitier
   c. Moses Gunn
   d. James Earl Jones

6. What kind of creature was Champion in the title of the popular 1950s series?

a. Dog
b. Cat
c. Bear
d. Horse

7. The first episode of which of these four hugely popular US TV staples was broadcast in 1959?

    a. Bonanza
    b. Mr. Ed
    c. I Love Lucy
    d. The Tonight Show

8. True or False? Future *Golden Girl* Betty White hosted her own daytime television chat show in 1952.

9. Which legendary actress won the Best Supporting Actress Oscar for her debut film role opposite Marlon Brando in 1954's *On the Waterfront*?

    a. Eva Marie Saint
    b. Kim Novak
    c. Shelley Winters
    d. Angela Lansbury

10. In 1955, *The Ed Sullivan* Show broadcast a live performance of what track, earning it a place in television history as the first rock 'n' roll song broadcast on a national television program?

    a. "Hound Dog"
    b. "Lucille"
    c. "Peggy Sue"
    d. "Rock Around the Clock"

ANSWERS

1. B. Thelma Ritter. A Tony and Emmy Award winner, Ritter never took home an Oscar despite a record-setting six Supporting Actress nominations for *All About Eve* (1950), *The Mating Season* (1951), *With a Song in My Heart* (1952), *Pickup on South Street* (1953), *Pillow Talk* (1959), and *Birdman of Alcatraz* (1962).

2. C. *Father Knows Best.* The series made its debut on NBC Radio in August 1949, before being picked up as a television sitcom five years later. Robert Young took the lead role in both series, with the television adaptation going on to run for a full six seasons.

3. B. *Psycho.* The 1950s is popularly seen as Hitchcock's heyday, as it was not only the decade in which he produced *Rear Window* (1954), *Vertigo* (1958), and *North by Northwest* (1959), but also *Strangers on a Train* (1950), *Dial M for Murder* (1954), and *To Catch a Thief* (1955). *Psycho* slipped into his filmography just a year too late to join his Golden Age in 1960 but was quickly followed by a string of other later successes, like *The Birds* (1963) and *Torn Curtain* (1966).

4. C. Doris Day. *The Man Who Knew Too Much* was another of Hitchcock's 1950s successes and the third of his four collaborations with James Stewart. Doris Day's track "Que Sera, Sera" from the movie went on to win the Academy Award for Best Original Song.

5. B. Sidney Poitier. Although Poitier lost out to David Niven for the Best Actor Oscar at the 31ˢᵗ Academy Awards in 1959, he went on to win the award just five years later for his role in 1962's *Lilies of the Field*. His victory made him the first Black performer in the Oscars' history to win a competitive award.

6. D. Horse. The on-screen companion of cowboy Gene Autry, Champion the Wonder Horse appeared in 79 movies and 91 episodes of *The Gene Autry Show* before taking the lead in 26 episodes of his own television series, *The Adventures of Champion*, in 1955.

7. A. *Bonanza*. First broadcast on September 12, 1959, *Bonanza* went on to run for 14 seasons and 431 episodes before ending in 1973. It remains the second longest-running Western series in American television history, after *Gunsmoke*.

8. True! *The Betty White Show* ran for three seasons from 1952–54. It had begun as *The Eddie Albert Show* (which was in turn a spinoff of the popular *Hollywood on Television* series, of which White was a cast member), but when Albert stepped down as host to pursue a career in Hollywood, White was promoted to host and took over Albert's role as producer.

9. A. Eva Marie Saint. Saint was just 30 years old at the time.

10. D. "Rock Around the Clock." Although *The Ed Sullivan Show* gets the credit for the song's first live broadcast on August 7, 1955, Bill Haley and His

Comets had also performed the track on an earlier episode of Milton Berle's *Texaco Star Theater* on May 31, 1955 (although this performance was partly a cappella and partly lip-synced).

DID YOU KNOW?

- RCA made history in the 1950s when it broadcast the first color television program on June 25, 1951.

- *I Love Lucy* was first broadcast on television in 1951. It would go on to make records across the US and worldwide, with four of its six seasons taking the title of America's most popular television program!

- Another of the decade's biggest television hits was Alfred Hitchcock *Presents*, which debuted in 1950 and ran for 361 episodes over the following ten years. Hitchcock himself, however, only directed 18 of them.

- Walt Disney continued to reign at the top of the worldwide box office in the 1950s, with his movies *Cinderella* (1950), *Peter Pan* (1953), and *Lady and the Tramp* (1955) grossing tens of millions of dollars between them. *Cinderella* alone grossed $20 million against a budget of just over $2 million and remains one of Disney's most profitable movies of all time!

- One of the biggest PR campaigns in Hollywood history was launched in 1959 to promote *Ben-Hur*. Costing almost $15 million - almost the same as the movie had cost to make! - the campaign included tie-in *Ben-Hur* candies, jewelry, neckties, toy armor, and even children's tricycles shaped like chariots!

MUSIC & POP CULTURE

THE 1950s

1. The Billboard Charts crowned its first Hot 100 Number One single in 1958. What was its title?
    a. "Cold Little Heart"
    b. "Hot Little Dog"
    c. "Poor Little Fool"
    d. "Sad Little Girl"

2. Which of these world-famous logos was first seen at a site in Phoenix, Arizona, in 1953?

    a. Mickey Mouse ears
    b. McDonald's golden arches
    c. Nike swoosh
    d. Marlboro man

3. Having previously been banned from the program, who appeared on *The Ed Sullivan Show* for the first time in 1956?

    a. The Beatles
    b. The Rolling Stones
    c. Bob Dylan
    d. Elvis Presley

4. In what year did Disneyland open in Anaheim, California?

    a. 1950
    b. 1952
    c. 1955
    d. 1959

5. Who had a hit with "It's Only Make Believe" in 1958?

    a. Tommy Edwards
    b. Conway Twitty
    c. Bobby Darin
    d. Lloyd Price

6. Starring Kathryn Grayson, Red Skelton, and Howard Keel, the 1952 MGM romantic comedy *Lovely to Look At* was an adaptation of what classic Jerome Kern Broadway musical?

a. Roberta
b. The Catch of the Season
c. Sally
d. Sweet Adeline

7. ...and in 1959, the Platters had a Number One hit in the US with what song from the same stage show?

a. "A Fine Romance"
b. "All The Things You Are"
c. "The Way You Look Tonight"
d. "Smoke Gets In Your Eyes"

8. Which high street store opened its first outlet in Quincy, Massachusetts, in 1950?

a. Dunkin' Donuts
b. Wendy's
c. Taco Bell
d. Panera

9. Who spent nine weeks at the top of the Billboard charts in 1959 with "Mack the Knife"?

a. Paul Anka
b. Frank Sinatra
c. Bobby Darin
d. Frankie Avalon

10. According to the lyrics of Elvis Presley's "Heartbreak Hotel," who is "dressed in black"?

a. Chambermaid
b. Desk clerk
c. Bellhop
d. Barman

ANSWERS

1. C. "Poor Little Fool." The classic country rock track was performed by Ricky Nelson, who held the Number One spot on the Billboard chart for two weeks. The song had been written by legendary songwriter Sharon Sheeley, who was just 15 at the time of its composition.

2. B. McDonald's golden arches. Established in 1940s, McDonald's became a franchise in the 1950s, with the first franchise site to bear the store's now iconic arched logo opening on the corner of Central Avenue and Indian School Road in Phoenix in 1953.

3. D. Elvis Presley. Sullivan had previously banned Elvis as his gyrating dance moves were considered indecent and in contravention of television's strict censorship laws. He quickly changed his mind when the singer - who was just 21 at the time - made an appearance on the rival *Steve Allen Show*, which beat Sullivan's show in the ratings. As a result, Elvis was offered a $50,000 fee for three guaranteed future appearances on *The Ed Sullivan Show*, the first of which was broadcast on September 9, 1956.

4. C. 1955. There was so much press surrounding the opening of Disneyland on Monday, July 18, 1955, that the first customers began queuing up at two o'clock in the morning!

5. B. Conway Twitty. The track not only topped the US Billboard chart but also reached the top spot in

Canada and the United Kingdom too. "It's Only Make Believe" later returned to the Top Ten in 1970, when it was covered by Glen Campbell.

6. A. *Roberta*. The big-budget adaptation of the 1933 Broadway hit had originally been intended as a vehicle for Judy Garland, Gene Kelly, and Frank Sinatra, but scheduling and budgeting conflicts led to Grayson, Skelton, and Keel taking the roles instead.

7. D. "Smoke Gets In Your Eyes." Jerome Kern had originally intended "Smoke Gets In Your Eyes" to be used during a tapdancing routine in *Show Boat*, but the plans were changed, and the song was shelved until *Roberta* debuted on Broadway in 1933. The Platters' version of the track spent three weeks at the top of the Billboard charts in January 1959 and was one of the year's biggest-selling singles.

8. A. Dunkin' Donuts. Operating merely under the name of Dunkin' since 2019, the first Dunkin' Donuts store was founded by entrepreneur Bill Rosenberg in Quincy, Massachusetts. Two years earlier, he had opened and run a smaller coffee and donut store under the name "Open Kettle" but renamed the brand when it expanded in 1950.

9. C. Bobby Darin. First reaching the top spot on October 5, "Mack the Knife" remained at Number One until mid-November, when it was replaced for just one week by The Fleetwoods' hit "Mr. Blue." It reclaimed the top position on November 23 and

remained there for a further three weeks to become the year's most successful single.

10. D. Desk clerk. As Elvis sings in the song's second verse, "The bellhop's tears keep flowin', and the desk clerk's dressed in black."

DID YOU KNOW?

- Elvis Presley received his first radio play this decade on July 8, 1953, when Memphis DJ Dewey Phillips played The King's hit "That's All Right" on his *Red, Hot, and Blue* radio show

- Among the many quintessential pop culture landmarks to make their debut in the 1950s, Pez candies first went on sale in the United States in 1952.

- *Village Voice* magazine first went on sale in the US in 1955.

- "Rock Around the Clock" became the biggest-selling single of the 1950s, shifting an estimated 15 million copies worldwide. It was also the first rock 'n' roll song to top the charts on both sides of the Atlantic: in the UK, the song became the first single in British chart history to sell one million units!

- The first Grammy Awards ceremony was held on May 4, 1959. Composer Henry Mancini took the inaugural Album of the Year award for his *Music from Peter Gunn*, while Italian singer Domenico Modugno won both Song and Record of the Year for his 1958 hit "Nel Blu Dipinto di Blu (Volare)." Other winners on the night included Ella Fitzgerald and Count Basie.

SPORTS

THE 1950s

1. The 1956 Summer Olympic Games were the first to be held in the Southern Hemisphere, and the first not to be held in either Europe or North America. Which Australian city hosted them?

   a. Sydney
   b. Melbourne
   c. Perth
   d. Brisbane

2. In 1953, who became the first team in baseball history to win five consecutive MLB World Series titles?

    a. New York Yankees
    b. Oakland Athletics
    c. Chicago White Sox
    d. Baltimore Orioles

3. Ben Hogan was a famous name in what sport in the 1950s?

    a. Football
    b. Swimming
    c. Athletics
    d. Golf

4. In fact,...Ben Hogan's domination of his sport in this decade was even more remarkable, given that he had previously suffered devastating injuries in a horse-riding accident. True or False?

5. What was introduced to NBA basketball matches in 1954?

    a. Orange ball
    b. Shot clock
    c. Three-point line
    d. Backboard

6. NBA star Frank Selvy set a college record in 1954 for scoring how many points in a single game of basketball?

    a. 50
    b. 70

c. 100
d. 120

7. Several records were set at the 1952 Olympic Games. But the host city itself also took an Olympic record - for what?

    a. Smallest host city
    b. First non-capital host city
    c. Northernmost host city
    d. First Games held on an island

8. In 1956, Althea Gibson became the first African American to win a Grand Slam tennis title. Which title did she take?

    a. Wimbledon
    b. US Open
    c. French Open
    d. Australian Open

9. Who held the world heavyweight boxing championship title from 1952 to 1956 and remains the only heavyweight champion in the sport's history to finish his career undefeated?

    a. Rocky Marciano
    b. Muhammad Ali
    c. Jersey Joe Walcott
    d. Ezzard Charles

10. In October 1957, which New York Yankees star pitched the only perfect game in World Series history?

    a. Bob Gibson
    b. Don Larsen

c. Nolan Ryan
d. Sandy Koufax

ANSWERS

1. B. Melbourne. Australia would later go on to host the Olympics again in 2000 when the Games were held in Sydney.

2. A. New York Yankees. In total, the Yankees took ten World Series titles in the 1940s and 50s, but their chain of five consecutive victories from 1949 to 1953 remains unsurpassed to this day. Completing their domination of the decade, they also won the 1956 and 1958 World Series titles, too.

3. D. Golf. Hogan won nine professional golf majors in his career, and he remains one of just five players in the sport's history to have won all four major tournaments: the Masters, both the British and US Open tournaments, and the PGA Championship.

4. False. In fact, Hogan was injured in an automobile accident, while driving home in thick fog in 1949. Having collided head-on with a Greyhound bus, Hogan broke several bones - including his ankle, collar bone, and his pelvis in two places—and was told by his doctors that he would never walk again. Incredibly, he defied all expectations to be named Golfer of the Year just 12 months after the crash and went on to win the 1950, 1951, and 1953 US Open competitions.

5. B. Shot clock. The 24-second shot clock was intended to increase the speed of the game. The sport's trademark orange ball was added in 1958, to make it

more visible during play, while the three-point line was added in the 1979–80 season. Backboards meanwhile have been part of the standard basketball hoop setup since the sport's earliest days, in the early 1900s.

6. C. 100. Selvy scored 100 points for Furman University in a game against Newberry College on February 13, 1954, becoming the only NCAA Division I player in history to do so.

7. C. Northernmost host city. The 1952 Summer Olympics were held in Helsinki, Finland. The city had originally been chosen to host the Games in 1940, but they were canceled due to World War II. The 1952 Games had originally been awarded to Tokyo, but when they had to withdraw due to the ongoing Second Sino-Japanese War, the Games were handed to Helsinki to make up for losing out the previous decade. At 60° north, and just 440 miles from the Arctic Circle, the city remains the northernmost in the world ever to have hosted the Summer Olympics.

8. C. French Open. Ranked Number One in the world for two consecutive years in 1957 and 1958, Gibson went on to win 11 Grand Slam titles in her career - five as a solo player (including back-to-back Wimbledon and US Open titles in 1957 and 1958), five in doubles tournaments, and one (also in the 1957 US Open) in the mixed doubles.

9. A. Rocky Marciano. As well as retiring undefeated, Marciano remains the only fighter in boxing history

to have defeated every opponent he ever came up against for the world heavyweight title, and he shares the title of the highest knockout-to-win percentage in world heavyweight title fights (85.71%) with the equally legendary Joe Louis.

10.B. Don Larsen. As well as being the only perfect game in the history of the World Series, Larsen's 1957 game was only the sixth perfect game since the inauguration of Major League Baseball.

DID YOU KNOW?

- 1950 marked the first time in history that Black players were allowed to compete in the NBA, paving the way for stars like Bill Russell to dominate the sport this decade.

- Equestrian events fell afoul of Australia's strict quarantine laws during the 1956 Olympics: while the rest of the Games were held in the southern hemisphere, all events featuring horses were held almost 10,000 miles away in Stockholm, Sweden!

- Boxing emerged as a truly worldwide sport in the 1950s, with Vic Toweel becoming South Africa's first world champion, Jimmy Carruthers becoming Australia's first world champion, Pascual Pérez doing the same for Argentina, Yoshio Shirai for Japan, and Hogan Bassey winning the first belt for Nigeria!

- Jersey Joe Walcott, meanwhile, became boxing's oldest heavyweight world champion in 1952 at the age of 37!

- Women's sport also broke out in the 1950s, with swimmer Florence Chadwick getting the decade off to a grand start when she swam the English Channel in 13 hours and 20 minutes on August 8, 1950, setting a new record time in the process!

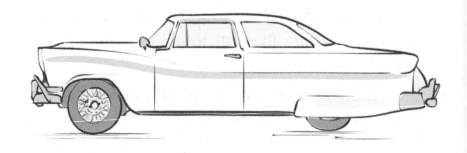

BONUS ROUND

THE 1950s

1. In 1950s America, James was the most popular boy's name of the decade, closely followed by Michael. What was the number one girl's name?
   a. Mary
   b. Alison
   c. Brenda
   d. Cynthia

2. The birth rate in the United States peaked in the 1950s. As of the 2020s, it is currently around 12 births per 1,000 people - but on average, what was it seven decades earlier?

a. 14
b. 17
c. 21
d. 24

3. On average, what you could expect to pay for a new car in early 1950s America?

    a. $1,000
    b. $2,200
    c. $4,500
    d. $8,000

4. Which US state updated the design of its flag in 1957, ahead of its centennial in 1958?

    a. Minnesota
    b. Florida
    c. Oregon
    d. New Hampshire

5. What was the average cost of a house in 1950s America?

    a. $3,000
    b. $7,000
    c. $12,000
    d. $21,000

6. Which of these comic strip characters made their debut in 1950?

    a. Huckleberry Hound
    b. Marmaduke
    c. Garfield
    d. Charlie Brown

7. The 1953 Oscars marked a milestone in the awards' history. What was it?
   a. First tie
   b. First female host
   c. First Supporting performance categories
   d. First live television broadcast

8. Which of these 1950s power couples wed at the bride's childhood home in Rhode Island on September 12, 1953?
   a. John F Kennedy and Jacqueline Bouvier
   b. Marilyn Monroe and Joe DiMaggio
   c. Frank Sinatra and Ava Gardner
   d. Tony Curtis and Janet Leigh

9. And on the subject of celebrity couples…how many times did Elizabeth Taylor tie the knot in the 1950s?
   a. Once
   b. Twice
   c. Three times
   d. Four times

10. The work of scientists James Watson, Francis Crick, Maurice Wilkins, and Rosalind Franklin unlocked the secrets of which of these previously unknown wonders in the 1950s?
   a. Black holes
   b. Microwaves
   c. DNA
   d. Pulsars

ANSWERS

1. A. Mary. In fact, Mary was the number one girl's name in the United States every year from 1880 until 1961!

2. D. 24. Incredibly, since the height of the post-war Baby Boom, the birth rate in the US has halved from a peak of 24.2 births per 1,000 three-quarters of a century ago!

3. B. $2,200. Cheap by modern standards, car prices had nevertheless risen sharply by the 1950s, thanks to postwar inflation.

4. A. Minnesota. Prior to 1957, the opposite sides of the Minnesotan flag had been different colors: one side white, the other bright blue. The 1957 redesign made the background of both sides solid navy blue, cheapening the manufacturing costs and lowering the weight of the flag itself.

5. B. $7,000. The median home price of a house in 1950 was $7,354 - around twice the average yearly household income.

6. D. Charlie Brown. The first *Peanuts* cartoon strip by Charles M Schulz appeared in newspapers on October 2, 1950.

7. D. First live television broadcast. The 25th Academy Awards were broadcast live on television to an audience of around 40 million people. Hosted by Bob Hope, the ceremony - which was split between

Hollywood and New York - was broadcast on NBC for a fee of $100,000.

8. A. John F Kennedy and Jacqueline Bouvier. In front of over 1,200 invited guests, the Kennedys were wed at Hammersmith Farm, the Victorian mansion and estate on Harrison Avenue in Newport, Rhode Island, where Jacqueline had grown up.

9. D. Four times. A full half of Elizabeth Taylor's eight marriages took place in this decade: Conrad Hilton, Jr. (1950–51), Michael Wilding (1952–57), Mike Todd (1957–58), and Eddie Fisher (1959–64).

10.C. DNA. Crick and Watson first outlined the double helix structure of the DNA molecule in 1953, with Crick and Wilkins going on to be awarded the 1962 Nobel Prize for Medicine for their work in unlocking the secrets of the genetic molecular structure in 1962.

DID YOU KNOW?

- In Great Britain, the traditional yearly royal Christmas broadcast was shown on television for the first time in the 1950s, with Queen Elizabeth II giving the first televised royal festive address on Christmas Day, 1957.

- There was no Miss America 1950 - because in that year the organization behind the pageant decided to post-date the title, so the 1950 winner, Yolande Betbeze, became Miss America 1951!

- Among the countless inventions and modern developments that appeared this decade were TV dinners (in 1953), fiber optics (1956), the barcode (1952), the hovercraft (1954), the Diners Club card (1950), nylon pantyhose (1959), and the Barbie doll (1959).

- Future Beatles bandmates John Lennon and Paul McCartney met for the first time as teenagers at a garden fete in Liverpool, England, in 1957.

- The post-war Baby Boom peaked in the United States in 1957, when over four-and-a-quarter million babies were born.

PART 2:
THE 1960s

IN THE NEWS

THE 1960s

1. One of these US agencies was founded in 1961. Which one?
   a. Peace Corps
   b. National Parks Authority
   c. Homeland Security
   d. CIA

2. What first did spacecraft *Freedom 7* achieve in 1961?
   a. First orbit of the Earth
   b. First American in space
   c. First safe return spaceflight of a dog
   d. First photograph of the dark side of the Moon

3. True or False? Martin Luther King's "I Have a Dream" speech took place three months after the assassination of President Kennedy.

4. Jack Ruby assassinated President Kennedy's rumored assassin Lee Harvey Oswald live on television in 1963. What was Ruby's occupation?

    a. Architect
    b. Orthodontist
    c. High school teacher
    d. Nightclub owner

5. The results of the US Supreme Court's 1966 *Miranda vs. Arizona* case changed the workings of what profession forever?

    a. Teaching
    b. Police service
    c. Nursing
    d. Journalism

6. The Bay of Pigs invasion and the construction of the Berlin Wall both happened in the same year in the 1960s. But which year was it?

    a. 1961
    b. 1964
    c. 1966
    d. 1978

7. After the assassination of President Kennedy in 1963, his vice president Lyndon Johnson had to be sworn in just two hours later...where?

    a. Paris, France

b. On board Air Force One

c. Camp David

d. The Everglades National Park

8. Which country underwent a major Cultural Revolution in the 1960s?

   a. Italy

   b. Mexico

   c. Brazil

   d. China

9. The so-called Six Day War broke out in 1967 - in what region of the world?

   a. Southern Europe

   b. Southeast Asia

   c. Middle East

   d. Central America

10. Three of these events took place in 1969. One of them did not. Which one?

   a. Moon landings

   b. Woodstock Festival

   c. Assassination of Martin Luther King

   d. Stonewall Riots

ANSWERS

1. A. Peace Corps. The Peace Corps was established by executive order of President Kennedy on March 1, 1961.

2. B. First American in space. Launched on May 5, 1961, Freedom 7 was piloted by NASA astronaut Alan Shepard whose solo 15-minute suborbital test flight - at a height of around 100 miles above the Earth's surface - made him the first American astronaut to travel into (and safely return from) space.

3. False. King delivered his "I Have a Dream" address on August 28, 1963, almost exactly three months *before* President Kennedy's assassination on November 22.

4. D. Nightclub owner. Born Jacob Rubenstein in Chicago, Ruby had relocated to Dallas in 1947 to help his sister, who ran a nightclub in the city. Over the years that followed, he went on to open a number of clubs and nightlife venues across the city.

5. B. Police service. The *Miranda vs. Arizona* case led to the ruling that law enforcement providers in the United States must warn a person of their constitutional rights before interrogating them, or else their statements cannot be used as evidence at their trial. The recitation of this rule at a person's

arrest remains known as the Miranda Rights to this day.

6. A. 1961. The failed landing at the Bay of Pigs in Cuba took place from April 17–20, 1961. Across in Europe, the border between East and West Germany was closed on August 13 - a date still known as Barbed Wire Sunday - and construction of a stone wall followed four days later.

7. B. On board Air Force One. Contrary to popular belief, Air Force One was not in the air as Johnson swore the oath of office but on the ground at Dallas Love Field airport. After the ceremony was complete, the plane returned the new president to Washington, DC.

8. D. China. The upheaval of China's great Cultural Revolution was launched by Mao Zedong in 1966 and lasted until his death in 1976.

9. C. Middle East. Also known as the Third Arab Israeli War, the Six Days War - fought between Israel and a coalition of surrounding Arab states, including Egypt, Syria, and Jordan - lasted from June 5 to June 10, 1967.

10. D. Assassination of Martin Luther King. King was assassinated in Memphis, Tennessee, on April 4, 1968. The Stonewall Riots took place on June 28, 1969; man walked on the Moon on July 20, 1969; and Woodstock opened its gates on August 15, 1969.

DID YOU KNOW?

- History was made in 1960 when the Trieste submersible - piloted by US Navy Lieutenant Donald Walsh and Jacques Piccard - descended to the bottom of the Mariana Trench, the lowest place on earth!

- The first televised presidential debate took place on September 26, 1960. As many as 70 million people tuned in around the country to watch White House hopefuls Vice President Richard Nixon and Senator John F Kennedy.

- Tragedy struck and headlines were made around the world on August 5, 1962, when Marilyn Monroe was found dead in her home.

- Alcatraz Prison in California was officially closed in 1963 when the cost of running the island institution proved too great to be maintained.

- Work was completed on St. Louis' monumental Gateway Arch in October 1965, when the two halves of the gigantic, curved structure were finally joined.

MOVIES & TV

THE 1960s

1. In 1962, Swiss actor Maximilian Schell won the Academy Award for Best Actor for his role in 1961's *Judgment at Nuremberg*. For only the sixth time in movie history, one of his costars was also nominated for the same award. Who was he?

    a. Laurence Olivier
    b. Peter O'Toole
    c. Spencer Tracy
    d. Christopher Plummer

2. In the 1960s sitcom *Bewitched*, what relation was Endora to the show's lead, Samantha?

    a. Sister
    b. Daughter
    c. Mother
    d. Mother-in-law

3. What hit 1960 movie was based on a novel by Howard Fast?

    a. The Hustler
    b. Breakfast At Tiffany's
    c. Psycho
    d. Spartacus

4. Which of these classic 1960s series was broadcast first?

    a. The Munsters
    b. I Dream of Jeannie
    c. Gilligan's Island
    d. The Dick Van Dyke Show

5. In 1960, moviemaker Otto Preminger gave which notorious Hollywood name his first onscreen credit in over ten years for his contribution to the movie *Exodus*?

    a. Dalton Trumbo
    b. José Ferrer
    c. Lester Cole
    d. Adrian Scott

6. Who starred as *Zorba the Greek* in 1964?

    a. Peter Sellers
    b. Anthony Perkins

c. Anthony Quinn

d. Kirk Douglas

7. What was the occupation of Larry Hagman's character Tony in the TV sitcom *I Dream of Jeannie*?

a. Architect

b. Astronaut

c. Accountant

d. Aircraft pilot

8. What was Marilyn Monroe's last completed movie?

a. Bus Stop

b. Some Like It Hot

c. The Misfits

d. Love Nest

9. In one of the biggest scandals of the time, who was fired from the set of *Valley of the Dolls* in 1967?

a. Judy Garland

b. Sophia Loren

c. Raquel Welch

d. Jayne Mansfield

10. True or False? Lucille Ball helped to produce the 1966 espionage series *Mission: Impossible*.

ANSWERS

1. C. Spencer Tracy. Dual Best Actor nods for the same movie have only occurred 12 times in Oscar history, but three of those times were for movies released in the 1960s: as well as *Judgment at Nuremberg*, both Richard Burton and Peter O'Toole were nominated for their performances in *Becket* (1964), and both Dustin Hoffman and Jon Voight went up against one another for *Midnight Cowboy* (1969). Unlike in 1962, however, none of the four were successful: Burton and O'Toole lost to Rex Harrison in *My Fair Lady*, and Hoffman and Voight lost to John Wayne in *True Grit*.

2. C. Mother. Endora was famously played by Agnes Moorehead, opposite Elizabeth Montgomery as Samantha.

3. D. *Spartacus*. *Psycho* was based on a novel by Robert Bloch, *The Hustler* was based on a novel by Walter Tevis, and *Breakfast at Tiffany's* was based on a novella by Truman Capote.

4. D. *The Dick Van Dyke Show*. *The Dick Van Dyke Show* debuted in 1961, whereas both *The Munsters* and *Gilligan's Island* were first broadcast in 1964, and *I Dream of Jeannie* followed on in 1965.

5. A. Dalton Trumbo. Screenwriter Dalton Trumbo was one of the original Hollywood Ten, who were blacklisted during the McCarthy era in Hollywood for their supposed ties to Communism. During this

time, Trumbo won two Academy Awards writing under the pseudonym Robert Rich but was unable to reveal his contribution to the movies and accept the awards.

6. C. Anthony Quinn. Already a two-time Oscar winner, Quinn was nominated for his fourth Academy Award for his performance as Alexis Zorba.

7. B. Astronaut.

8. C. *The Misfits*. Monroe was midway through filming one more movie, 1962's *Something's Got To Give*, when she died. The film was later abandoned.

9. A. Judy Garland. The movie had been intended to pave the way for Garland's Hollywood comeback, but when her personal troubles became too much she was fired from the set and Susan Hayward took her role instead.

10. True! *Mission: Impossible* was financed by Desilu Productions, the production company founded and co-owned by Ball and her then-husband Desi Arnaz. As well as financing her own show, Ball's work through Desilu also helped to bring *Mannix*, *Star Trek*, and *The Untouchables* to the small screen.

DID YOU KNOW?

- Despite initially lukewarm reviews, 1965's *The Sound of Music* went on to become the most successful movie of all time this decade, earning a worldwide gross of $286 million. *The Sound of Music* also went on to be nominated for a record ten Oscars (tying that year with *Doctor Zhivago*), winning five in total. Julie Andrews missed out on her second Best Actress award to Zhivago's Julie Christie, while Christopher Plummer's performance in the film was famously snubbed and did not receive a nomination at all!

- *Cleopatra*, starring Elizabeth Taylor and Richard Burton, had a famously troubled production and ended up going massively over-budget due to issues both on and off screen. When Taylor's health broke down early during shooting, production was suspended with just ten minutes of usable footage recorded! The budget eventually spiraled to $31 million (equivalent to almost $300 million today!), making it the most expensive movie of all time at that point.

- Television shows that made their debut this decade included *Star Trek* (1966), *Doctor Who* (1963), *Mission: Impossible* (1968), *The Andy Griffith Show* (1960), and *Hawaii Five-O* (1968).

- Adam West's television series *Batman* was also broadcast this decade, with all 120 episodes over all three series shown from 1966 to 1968. It remained the longest-running live-action superhero series in television history for the next four decades, until it was surpassed by *Superman* serial *Smallville* in 2007!

- The first star on the Hollywood Walk of Fame - that of 1960s starlet Joanne Woodward - was unveiled on February 9, 1960.

MUSIC & POP CULTURE

THE 1960s

1. Which US folk singer was famously arrested in an anti-draft protest outside an army recruitment center in Oakland, California, in 1967?
    a. Judy Collins
    b. Joan Baez
    c. Dolly Parton
    d. Emmylou Harris
2. In 1962, drummer Pete Best was replaced in the lineup of what iconic band?
    a. The Rolling Stones
    b. The Byrds

c. The Beach Boys

d. The Beatles

3. True or False? The Doors were banned from appearing on *The Ed Sullivan Show* in 1967 after front man Jim Morrison refused to fasten his shirt on screen.

4. Widely considered one of the greatest albums of all time, which American blues musician recorded his acclaimed *Live at the Regal* album in 1964?

a. Muddy Waters

b. BB King

c. Buddy Guy

d. Freddie King

5. The Beatles had 18 Billboard Number One singles in the 1960s. Which supergroup of the era ranks second, with 12?

a. The Beach Boys

b. The Crystals

c. The Supremes

d. The Rolling Stones

6. Who sang the theme tune to the 1963 James Bond movie *From Russia With Love*?

a. Tom Jones

b. Shirley Bassey

c. Matt Monro

d. Nancy Sinatra

7. In what year did Aretha Franklin have a Number One hit with "Respect"?

a. 1961

b. 1963

c. 1967

d. 1969

8. The biggest-selling single of 1969 contains the lines, "When I kissed you, girl I knew how sweet a kiss could be / Like the summer sunshine, pour your sweetness over me." What is it?

    a. "I Can't Help Myself"

    b. "Sugar, Sugar"

    c. "Get Back"

    d. "Honk Tonk Woman"

9. The songwriting and music production trio known as Holland–Dozier–Holland are associated with what 1960s genre?

    a. Rock 'n' roll

    b. Motown

    c. Jazz

    d. Latin

10. In what month of 1969 did the Woodstock music festival take place?

    a. April

    b. June

    c. August

    d. September

ANSWERS

1. B. Joan Baez. Baez was arrested along with around 70 other Vietnam War protesters - including her mother!

2. D. The Beatles. Known as The Fifth Beatle, Best was replaced by Ringo Starr when the Beatles' producer, George Martin, decided the band needed a more experienced drummer in their studio recording sessions.

3. False. Actually, the disagreement was over the band refusing to change the lyrics to their hit "Light My Fire": the show's producers wanted Morrison to avoid using the line "Girl we couldn't get any higher" on television because of its overt reference to drug use. Although the band at first agreed to the alteration, they later changed their mind and insisted their performance of the song be recorded as intended, keeping the lyrics intact. As a result, the producers tore up the band's lucrative contract for six appearances on the show and banned them from ever appearing on the show again!

4. B. BB King.

5. C. The Supremes. The Supremes first hit the top spot with "Where Did Our Love Go" in 1964 and followed that up with another 11 chart-toppers inside just five years: "Baby Love and Come See About Me" in 1964; "Stop! In the Name of Love," "Back in My Arms Again," and "I Hear a

Symphony" in 1965; "You Can't Hurry Love" and "You Keep Me Hangin' On" in 1966; "Love Is Here and Now You're Gone" and "The Happening" in 1967; "Love Child" in 1968; and "Someday We'll Be Together" in 1969. The group's extraordinary domination of the decade saw them spend a full 22 weeks at Number One on the Billboard charts - tying them with Elvis Presley!

6. C. Matt Monro. The song was written by British composer and songwriter Lionel Bart, who is best known for writing the musical *Oliver!*

7. C. 1967. Incredibly, the track was Franklin's only Number One of the entire decade.

8. B. "Sugar, Sugar." The Archies' only US Number One, "Sugar, Sugar" also hit the top spot around the world - including in the UK and Canada - and remains the biggest-selling bubblegum hit pop song in music history.

9. B. Motown. Lamont Dozier and brothers Brian and Eddie Holland are responsible for a great many classic Motown songs, including hits for Martha and the Vandellas, the Four Tops, Marvin Gaye, and ten of the Supremes' 12 US Number Ones.

10. C. August. The event was held from August 15 to 18, 1969, on Max Yasgur's dairy farm in Bethel, 40 miles outside of the New York town of Woodstock.

DID YOU KNOW?

- The biggest-selling song in the US in the 1960s was Chubby Checker's "The Twist." It also made history for becoming the first track to top the charts on two separate occasions: originally charting on the hit parade in the summer of 1960, the song returned to the top slot two years later in January 1962. The same feat would not happen again for nearly 60 years, when Mariah Carey's "All I Want For Christmas Is You" returned to the top spot in 2020.

- Aretha Franklin won the first of her record-setting 18 Grammy Awards in 1968, taking two Rhythm and Blues Awards for her track "Respect." She would go on to win the Grammy Legend Award in 1991, the Lifetime Achievement Award in 1994, and the Person of the Year Award in 2008.

- The Beatles had their first US Number One and million-selling single in 1967, reaching the top spot with "Love Me Do." Oddly, the song was not as big a hit on home turf: in the UK, the song peaked at Number 17 on the chart!

- In 1968, Otis Redding's "(Sittin' On) The Dock Of The Bay" became the first posthumous Number One single in the United States: recorded just three days before Redding's death in a plane crash in December 1967, it sold three million copies on its release the following year and remains Redding's only chart-topper.

- The Beatles famously gave the last public performance of their career on the rooftop of their Apple Corps building in London on January 30, 1969. The concert was ended after 42 minutes, when the police arrived and told the band to keep the noise down!

SPORTS

THE 1960s

1. Which Yankees star struck his 61st season home run on the last day of the 1960–61 MLB season, January 1, 1961, breaking Babe Ruth's record that had stood since 1927?

    a. Roger Maris
    b. Mickey Mantle
    c. Mel Stottlemyre
    d. Tom Tresh

2. Which European capital city hosted the 1960 Summer Olympic Games?

    a. Rome

b. Paris

c. London

d. Amsterdam

3. Who defeated the Kansas City Chiefs in the very first Super Bowl in 1967?

  a. San Francisco 49ers
  b. Oakland Raiders
  c. Dallas Cowboys
  d. Green Bay Packers

4. In what winter sport were Czech brother and sister pairing Otto and Maria Jelinek famous names in the 1960s?

  a. Skiing
  b. Curling
  c. Figure skating
  d. Speed skating

5. Which 1960s MLB star was known as "The Commerce Comet"?

  a. Mickey Mantle
  b. Luis Arroyo
  c. Bobby Richardson
  d. Héctor López

6. On March 2, 1962, basketball legend Wilt Chamberlain single-handedly scored how many points in a single NBA game, setting a record that still stands to this day?

  a. 50
  b. 80

c. 100

d. 120

7. True or False? Bill Mazeroski hit a home run to secure victory for the Pittsburgh Pirates over the New York Yankees in the 1960 World Series - and it remains the only time such a finish has even happened in an MLB final.

8. How many gold medals did track and field legend Wilma Rudolph win at the 1960s Olympics?

    a. One

    b. Two

    c. Three

    d. Four

9. Who was named MVP in both of the first two Super Bowl championships, in 1967 and 1968?

    a. Bart Starr

    b. Joe Namath

    c. Len Dawson

    d. Chuck Howley

10. NBA legend Kareem Abdul-Jabbar made his professional basketball debut in 1969, playing for what team?

    a. Los Angeles Lakers

    b. Milwaukee Bucks

    c. Boston Celtics

    d. Golden State Warriors

ANSWERS

1. A. Roger Maris. Maris' record - which in turn stood until 1998 - remains controversial, as he broke Ruth's longstanding record of a total of 60 home runs in a season only when the number of season games was increased from 154 to 162.

2. A. Rome. The 1960 Games were also the first time in history that the Olympic and Paralympic Games were held in the same city at the same time. Rome had previously been due to host the Summer Olympics in 1908 but had to turn the responsibility down after a devastating eruption of Mount Vesuvius in 1906.

3. D. Green Bay Packers. The Packers defeated the Chiefs 35–10.

4. C. Figure skating. The Jelineks family were well-known business owners in mid-20th-century Czechoslovakia but were persecuted by the Gestapo during Germany's occupation of the country during World War II and again following the later Communist coup. The family fled to Switzerland, and then to Canada, and Otto and Maria Jelinek represented Canada when they won gold at the first World Figure Skating Championships in 1962 - which were held in the Czech capital, Prague.

5. A. Mickey Mantle. The nickname commemorated Mantle's childhood town of Commerce, Oklahoma.

6. C. 100. Chamberlain's record saw his Philadelphia Warriors secure an easy victory over the New York Knicks.

7. True!

8. C. Three. Rudolph took gold in the women's 100m, 200m, and 4 × 100 m relay. Her achievement to establish herself as an athletic legend was even more remarkable given that she had overcome polio as a child.

9. A. Bart Starr. Only six players in history have won the Super Bowl MVP title on more than one occasion, of which Starr was the first.

10. D. Milwaukee Bucks. Kareem Abdul-Jabbar was selected for the 1969 NBA draft by the Bucks and remained with the team until he moved to the Lakers in 1975.

DID YOU KNOW?

- On February 10, 1962, Jim Beatty became the first person to run the mile indoors in under four minutes, reaching a time of 3:58.9 in Los Angeles.

- In the 1960s, Satchel Paige became the oldest professional MLB baseball player in history, when he stepped out on the field for the final time in 1966 at the age of 59!

- In 1964, Masanori Murakami made history as the first Japanese baseball player to appear in the Major League when he appeared for the San Francisco Giants.

- In 1966, golfing legend Jack Nicolaus became the first player in history to win back-to-back Masters titles.

- Muhammad Ali became heavyweight champion in 1964 and maintained the title until 1970 - but was officially stripped of the title and had his boxing license removed when he refused the draft during the Vietnam War.

BONUS ROUND

THE 1960s

1. What was the most popular boy's name in the United States in the 1960s?

    a. Brian
    b. Thomas
    c. Michael
    d. Jeffrey

2. ...and after it had held the top spot for more than 80 years, what name replaced Mary as the most popular girl's name in the United States in 1961?

    a. Karen
    b. Pamela
    c. Joan
    d. Lisa

3. In his presidential campaign in the early 1960s, John F Kennedy had promised a wide-ranging social, legal, and political agenda meant as a follow-up and update to President Roosevelt's New Deal. What was it known as?

    a. The New Times
    b. The New Frontier
    c. The New World
    d. The New Movement

4. In what field did Mary Quant become a famous name in the 1960s?

    a. Sport
    b. Music
    c. Filmmaking
    d. Fashion

5. Taking to the stage at around half past eight on a rainy Monday evening, who was the last act to perform at Woodstock?

    a. Bob Dylan
    b. Janis Joplin
    c. Jimi Hendrix
    d. Eric Clapton

6. What was the average price of a house in 1960s America?

    a. Just under $12,000
    b. Just under $32,000
    c. Just under $52,000
    d. Just under $72,000

7. Fashion star Hubert de Givenchy famously created which of these quintessential 60s outfits?
    a. Audrey Hepburn's black dress in *Breakfast at Tiffany's*
    b. Julie Andrews' shoes in *Mary Poppins*
    c. Janet Leigh's brassiere in *Psycho*
    d. Faye Dunaway's beret hat in *Bonnie and Clyde*
8. The best-selling book of 1961 was *The Agony and the Ecstasy*. Who wrote it?
    a. Morris West
    b. Saul Bellow
    c. Leon Uris
    d. Irving Stone
9. ...and which famous artist was the subject of the book?
    a. Canaletto
    b. Michelangelo
    c. Da Vinci
    d. Renoir
10. At what time of day, in Eastern Daylight Time, did Neil Armstrong step onto the surface of the Moon in 1969?
    a. 9.17 a.m.
    b. 12.17 p.m.
    c. 4.17 p.m.
    d. 8.17 p.m.

ANSWERS

1. C. Michael. More than 830,000 Michaels were born in the US in the 60s, followed by David (730,000) and John (713,000) in second and third place.

2. D. Lisa. The name Lisa saw an extraordinary surge in popularity in the 1960s, having been ranked a relatively lowly 37th in the previous decade. In the 1950s, 95,000 Lisas were born, but a decade later that number had risen to a staggering 497,000!

3. B. The New Frontier. An ambitious package of laws and policies meant to rid Kennedy's America of injustice of all kinds, the New Frontier sadly faltered when many of its most progressive aims failed to win the support of southern Democrats.

4. D. Fashion. Dame Mary Quant was a leading part of the Swinging 60s fashion scene in London at the time and is one of the fashion designers said to be responsible for groundbreaking styles like the mini skirt and hotpants.

5. C. Jimi Hendrix. The bad weather had dampened the crowd's spirits by the time Hendrix took to the stage, so that from a peak of over 440,000 attendees at the height of the festival, only an estimated 30,000 people had stuck around to see Hendrix - many of whom left while he was still performing!

6. A. Just under $12,000. The median house price in 1960 was just $11,900 - equivalent to around $105,000 today.

7. A. Audrey Hepburn's black dress in *Breakfast at Tiffany's*. Three copies of Hepburn's famous "Little Black Dress" were made for the movie, one of which was sold to a private collector at auction in 2006 for £467,000 (equivalent to more than $975,000 today!)

8. D. Irving Stone.

9. B. Michelangelo. Stone had earlier had another best-seller with *Lust for Life*, his biographical novel about the life of the artist Vincent van Gogh, in 1934.

10. 4.17 p.m. Or 8.17 p.m. in GMT (UTC).

DID YOU KNOW?

- Among the countless modern inventions that debuted in the 1960s were the computer mouse (in 1960), the liquid crystal display or LCD (1968), MRI medical scanning (1969), and the birth control pill (1960).

- In 1962, the Beatles performed an early audition for Decca Records executives...but the band were not signed up and were instead told that guitar-centered groups are "on the way out"!

- Long before he stepped foot on the Moon, Neil Armstrong established a career as a NASA test pilot - and in 1962, flew the hypersonic research plane X-15 to a height of 25 miles above the Earth's surface!

- According to the *Oxford English Dictionary*, some new slang words that came into popular use in the 1960s include *in* (meaning "fashionable"), *fab* (short for "fabulous"), *grotty* and *grody* (meaning "dirty" or "unpleasant"), and *knock-out* (as an expression of excellence).

- Winston Churchill died at the age of 90 on January 25, 1965. He was given a full state funeral in the United Kingdom - the first for a non-royal in three decades - attended by representatives of more than 100 countries. The official procession through the streets of London attracted more than 300,000 spectators, making Churchill's the largest state funeral in British history.

PART 3:
THE 1970S

IN THE NEWS
THE 1970s

1. In 1972, President Richard Nixon became the first sitting president in American history to visit what country?
   a. South Africa
   b. Czechoslovakia
   c. Venezuela
   d. China

2. True or False? Margaret Thatcher, who was elected in 1979, was the United Kingdom's first female prime minister.

3. The so-called "Nixon Shock" of 1971 referred to a series of upheavals that affected what element of American society?

   a. Economy
   b. Justice system
   c. Electoral college
   d. Medical care

4. In 1972, which Apollo mission became the last to visit the Moon?

   a. Apollo 14
   b. Apollo 15
   c. Apollo 16
   d. Apollo 17

5. ...and the following year, NASA launched America's first permanent space station. What was its name?

   a. Mir
   b. ISS
   c. Skylab
   d. Genesis

6. The Watergate scandal was made public in the summer of 1972, when a team of how many burglars were apprehended and arrested at the Watergate office-apartment-complex on June 17?

   a. Four
   b. Five

c. Six

d. Seven

7. The 26th Amendment to the United States Constitution was ratified on July 1, 1971. What did it affect?

a. Voting age

b. Taxation

c. Presidential terms

d. Order of political succession

8. Jimmy Carter became the United States' 39th president in 1977. Who became his vice president?

a. Nelson Rockefeller

b. Spiro Agnew

c. Gerald Ford

d. Walter Mondale

9. In what year of the 1970s did the Three Mile Island nuclear disaster take place?

a. 1971

b. 1974

c. 1977

d. 1979

10.In 1978, the United States Senate voted to turn the Panama Canal over to Panamanian control - in what year?

a. 1979

b. 1999

c. 2020

d. 2050

ANSWERS

1. D. China. Despite his strong and longstanding anti-Communist stance, Nixon became the first president to visit mainland China, on a week-long state visit to Mao Zedong from February 21 to 28, 1972. A handful of earlier presidents had visited China both before and after their time in office: Ulysses S Grant visited the country as part of a world tour after leaving office; Herbert Hoover lived in China long before his presidency, from 1899 to 1901; and Dwight D Eisenhower made a state visit to the island of Taiwan in 1960.

2. True. In fact, Mrs. Thatcher was the first female leader in the United Kingdom for 258 years, since the very first prime minister was given the title way back in 1721 under King George I.

3. A. Economy. In 1971, President Nixon ended the supremacy of the United States Gold Standard and introduced a series of wage freezes, price freezes, and import surcharges, all in response to rising inflation. The outcome of his wide-ranging economic measures became known as the Nixon Shock.

4. D. Apollo 17.

5. C. Skylab. The only space station to date operated exclusively by the United States, Skylab was launched on May 14 and remained in operation and occupied in orbit above the Earth for the next 171

days. After being used by a rotating series of four teams of astronomical research scientists, the Skylab mission came to an end in the fall of 1973 and remained abandoned for the next six years. Finally, as its orbit gradually decayed, it reentered the Earth's atmosphere and disintegrated above the Indian Ocean in the summer of 1979.

6. B. Five. The five men were Virgilio Gonzalez, Bernard Barker, James McCord, Eugenio Martinez, and Frank Sturgis. They were accused of attempted burglary, as well as telephone tapping and other communications eavesdropping.

7. A. Voting age. Prior to 1971, the voting age in the United States had been limited to 21-year-olds, but when the Vietnam draft was extended to 18-year-olds, a campaign to lower the electoral age too quickly gathered momentum. Proposed by Congress on March 23, the amendment was ratified by the House of Representatives, by a margin of 401 votes to 19 in favor of the proposed amendment.

8. D. Walter Mondale. Mondale - America's 42nd vice president, and the fourth of the 1970s - later ran for the presidency himself but lost to Ronald Reagan in the 1984 election.

9. D. 1979. A partial meltdown at the Three Mile Island Nuclear Generating Station in Londonderry, Pennsylvania, the disaster occurred early on the morning of March 28, 1979.

10. B. 1999.

DID YOU KNOW?

- Environmental protections took a step forward in 1970, with the unanimous passing of the *Clean Air Act* in the Senate, and the formation of the Environmental Protection Agency under President Nixon.

- Amtrak was officially established by Congress in 1970 and took over the operation of America's previous rail companies the following year. In the two decades prior to that, the number of operating trains in the United States fell by 95% to just 450 individual trains by the 1970s.

- The world's first barcode was scanned on a packet of Wrigley's chewing gum on June 26, 1974.

- A true daredevil stunt made headlines around the world on August 7, 1974, when Philippe Petit successfully (and repeatedly) walked a highwire strung between the Twin Towers of the World Trade Center in New York City. As soon as he returned to ground level, he and his collaborator were arrested.

- Ted Bundy was arrested on August 18, 1975, initially for evading a police officer. In the aftermath of the arrest, police found handcuffs, a ski mask, and pantyhose with eyes cut out among his belongings - eventually leading to him being connected to more than 30 murders.

MOVIES & TV

THE 1970s

1. In 1970, the first X-rated Best Picture Oscar winner in movie history was crowned at the 42nd Academy Awards. What was it?
   a. The Exorcist
   b. A Clockwork Orange
   c. Midnight Cowboy
   d. Taxi Driver

2. True or False? *Jaws* was the highest grossing movie of the decade in the 1970s.

3. What 1975 movie won all five major Oscars - the awards for Best Picture, Best Actor, Best Actress, Best Director, and Screenplay - at the 48th Academy Awards?

   a. Dog Day Afternoon
   b. One Flew Over the Cuckoo's Nest
   c. Barry Lyndon
   d. Farewell, My Lovely

4. Which of these Hollywood moguls died in the 1970s?

   a. Samuel Goldwyn
   b. Louis B Mayer
   c. David O Selznick
   d. Alfred Hitchcock

5. When he was awarded an honorary Oscar in 1972, which British movie-making legend received a record-breaking 12-minute standing ovation at the Academy Awards?

   a. Laurence Olivier
   b. David Lean
   c. Charlie Chaplin
   d. Richard Attenborough

6. Which of these 1970s television sitcoms was first shown in the 1970s?

   a. Cheers
   b. Diff'rent Strokes

c. Full House

d. Growing Pains

7. Which of these superheroes became one of the biggest cinema stars of 1978?

    a. Batman

    b. Spider-Man

    c. Superman

    d. Captain America

8. What classic television drama series was first broadcast as a two-hour feature length pilot movie in the spring of 1974, with its first shorter 50-minute episode following on in September of the same year?

    a. Little House on the Prairie

    b. Buck Rogers in the 25th Century

    c. Dallas

    d. The Waltons

9. As part of an infamously troubled year-long shoot, Marlon Brando was paid an immense fee for his appearance in the 1979 Vietnam War epic *Apocalypse Now*. How much was he paid for barely ten minutes of screen time?

    a. $100,000

    b. $500,000

    c. $1 million

    d. $2 million

10. 1978's adaptation of Agatha Christie's *Death on the Nile* had a famously A-list all-star cast. Which of

these legendary actresses did NOT appear in the cast's lineup?

a. Maggie Smith
b. Bette Davis
c. Angela Lansbury
d. Lauren Bacall

ANSWERS

1. C. *Midnight Cowboy.* Coincidentally, *Midnight Cowboy* became the first X-rated Best Picture Oscar winner one year after the Academy crowned its first G-rated Best Picture winner, *Oliver!*

2. False. *Star Wars* took the global box office by storm this decade, earning a massive three-quarters of a billion dollars on its release in 1977.

3. B. *One Flew Over the Cuckoo's Nest.* The "Big Five" clean sweep has only happened three times in Oscar history, first with 1934's *It Happened One Night,* and then again with 1991's *Silence of the Lambs.* Alongside the likes of Jack Nicholson's Best Actor award, Louise Fletcher's Best Actress Oscar, and the first of Miloš Forman's two Best Director Academy Awards, *One Flew Over the Cuckoo's Nest* was nominated for nine Oscars in total, with Brad Dourif missing out on the Best Supporting Actor award to George Burns in *The Sunshine Boys.*

4. A. Samuel Goldwyn. Polish-born movie producer Samuel Goldwyn - the G in MGM Studios - died in Los Angeles on January 31, 1974, at the age of 91. His colleague Louis B Mayer died in 1957; *Gone With The Wind* filmmaker David O Selznick died in 1965; and British movie legend Sir Alfred Hitchcock died in 1980.

5. C. Charlie Chaplin. The event was especially important as it marked Chaplin's first visit to the

United States in over 20 years and came 43 years after his first honorary Oscar in 1929. In total, Chaplin was awarded three Oscars in his career - earning his third in 1973 when he won Best Original Score for the re-release of his classic movie, *Limelight*.

6. B. *Diff'rent Strokes*. *Diff'rent Strokes* was first broadcast in 1978 and ran for eight seasons and 189 episodes until 1986. *Cheers* followed on in 1982, *Growing Pains* in 1985, and *Full House* in 1987.

7. C. Superman. Richard Donner's *Superman*, starring Christopher Reeve, was the most expensive movie ever made at the time, but it went on to earn almost six times its $55 million budget on its release in 1978.

8. A. *Little House on the Prairie*. The show went on to run for nine seasons and over 200 episodes, coming to an end in 1983.

9. D. $2 million. Brando arrived late, unprepared, and overweight for the shoot and did not get on with his costar, Dennis Hopper, and refused to be on set with him at the same time. As well as pocketing a $2 million fee for just four weeks on set (and ten minutes on screen!) Brandon was offered a further 10% of the movie's gross, and eventually earned around $9 million - equivalent to $38.5 million today - in total!

10. D. Lauren Bacall. Bacall had, however, earlier appeared in 1974's acclaimed adaptation of Christie's *Murder on the Orient Express*.

DID YOU KNOW?

- A true television scandal rocked the nation's sets in 1971 when a longstanding feud between Norman Mailer and Gore Vidal led to the pair fighting on the December 5 episode of *The Dick Cavett Show*. Backstage, the fight reached a peak when Mailer headbutted Vidal!

- HBO debuted this decade and became television's first premium cable channel on November 8, 1972.

- The world's first reality television show premiered this decade, when PBS' *An American Family* - debuted on January 11, 1973. The series, which told the real-life stories of a Californian family, the Louds, quickly attracted an audience of millions of viewers.

- One of the most popular shows in American television history debuted in 1974 when the first episode of *Happy Days* was broadcast on January 15. It would run for another decade, with 11 seasons and 255 episodes!

- This decade, 1975's biggest hit movie, Steven Spielberg's *Jaws*, became cinema's first "blockbuster": fast-paced, exciting, and leading to repeated viewings among the audience, it was seen as kickstarting the Blockbuster Era of cinema, which has continued to this day!

MUSIC & POP CULTURE

THE 1970s

1. Which company introduced Betamax tapes - the world's first commercially successful home video recording unit - in 1975?

   a. Samsung
   b. Sony
   c. Hitachi
   d. Siemens

2. Which of these classic Fleetwood Mac tracks is NOT found on their 1977 album *Rumours*?

   a. "The Chain"

b. "Go Your Own Way"

c. "Don't Stop"

d. "Sisters of the Moon"

3. Elvis Presley released his last original studio album - his 24th overall - just two months before his death, in June 1977. What was its title?

    a. Good Times

    b. Moody Blue

    c. Promised Land

    d. From Elvis Presley Boulevard, Memphis, Tennessee

4. In 2016, Pitchfork listed the 200 greatest tracks of the 1970s. Which of these was the only artist to have two tracks ranked in the Top 10?

    a. ABBA

    b. Michael Jackson

    c. David Bowie

    d. Prince

5. "Bad dreams in the night / They told me I was going to lose the fight" is a line from what classic 1970s single?

    a. "Tangled Up in Blue"

    b. "Wuthering Heights"

    c. "SOS"

    d. "What's Going On"

6. Legendary rock guitarist Jimi Hendrix died on September 18, 1970. Legendary singer and songwriter Janis Joplin died just a matter of weeks

later, on October 4, 1970. How old were they both at the time of their untimely deaths?

a. 24
b. 27
c. 32
d. 35

7. Which of these 1970s hits charted the earliest in the decade?

a. "Don't Stop 'til You Get Enough"
b. "Jolene"
c. "London Calling"
d. "Broken English"

8. Who is the oldest member of ABBA?

a. Agnetha Fältskog
b. Anni-Frid Lyngstad
c. Benny Andersson
d. Björn Ulvaeus

9. True or False? Elton John's classic 1970 hit single "Your Song" was first released by US rock band Three Dog Night, before Elton himself released his own recording of it a few months later.

10. The Bee Gees began a record-setting streak of six consecutive Billboard Number One singles in 1977 - with which track?

a. "Jive Talkin'"
b. "You Should Be Dancing"
c. "How Deep Is Your Love"
d. "The Woman in You"

ANSWERS

1. B. Sony. Despite having a better picture quality, Betamax was eventually ousted as the world's standard videotape format by VHS, which outdid it by allowing for longer recordings.

2. D. "Sisters of the Moon." "The Chain," "Go Your Own Way," and "Don't Stop" were among the six *Rumours* tracks released as singles. "Sisters of the Moon" was a single released from Fleetwood Mac's 1979 follow-up album, *Tusk*.

3. B. *Moody Blue*. The album contained a mixture of live recordings and studio recordings and featured the four tracks - "Way Down," "Pledging My Love," "It's Easy for You," and "He'll Have To Go" - recorded in Elvis' final studio sessions at Graceland in the fall of 1976.

4. C. David Bowie. Bowie came in sixth with his 1977 hit "Heroes," and first with 1971's "Life on Mars." His tracks "Young Americans" and "Changes" also made the list, at numbers 44 and 21. respectively.

5. B. "Wuthering Heights." Those lines open the bridge to Kate Bush's classic 1978 hit.

6. B. 27. Hendrix and Joplin are some of the most infamous members of rock 'n' roll's so-called 27 Club - an ever-growing list of musicians and artists who have passed away tragically young, at the age of just 27. As well as Jimi Hendrix and Janis Joplin, other "Club" members include their fellow 60s and

70s music stars Brian Jones of the Rolling Stones (who died the previous year, 1969) and Jim Morrison of the Doors (who died the following year, 1971). More recent members include Nirvana front man Kurt Cobain (who passed away in 1994), and Grammy winner Amy Winehouse (in 2011).

7. B. "Jolene." Dolly Parton's classic hit charted in 1973, whereas Michael Jackson's "Don't Stop 'til You Get Enough," "London Calling" by The Clash, and Marianne Faithful's "Broken English" were all released in 1979.

8. D. Björn Ulvaeus. Ulvaeus is just a few months older than Anni-Frid Lyngstad (known to fans as Frida), who were born in April and November of 1945, respectively. Lyngstad is a year older than her fellow bandmate (and former husband) Benny Andersson, who was born in December 1946, and five years older than her fellow vocalist, Agnetha Fältskog, who was born in April 1950.

9. True! Elton John had been the band's opening act on their recent tour and allowed them to record it as an unreleased track on their 1970 album *It Ain't Easy* before he released it on his second self-titled album - and later as a single - a month later, in April 1970.

10.C. "How Deep Is Your Love. How Deep Is Your Love" was followed consecutively at Number One on the Billboard charts by "Stayin' Alive" (also in 1977), "Night Fever" and "Too Much Heaven" (in

1978), and "Tragedy and Love You Inside Out" (in 1979).

DID YOU KNOW?

- 1970 was the year that Diana Ross and the Supremes performed their last concert together, on January 14 in Las Vegas. Ross soon afterward departed the group to embark on her successful solo career.

- Another music legend stepped out this decade when a band called the Stilettos broke apart and its female singer formed a new band called Angel and the Snake - before later changing the band's name to...Blondie!

- In the world of pop culture, feminist writing boomed in the 1970s following the publication of the first edition of *Ms.* magazine in December 1971.

- Developed by Atari, the world's first commercially successful arcade game *Pong* arrived in amusements and games centers this decade, in November 1972.

- On January 14, 1973, Elvis Presley became the first entertainer in history to hold a live broadcast via satellite, when his *Aloha from Hawaii* concert was shown across the United States - to a larger audience than the Moon Landing of 1969!

SPORTS

THE 1970s

1. In 1974, Hank Aaron broke Babe Ruth's home run record, when he struck his 715th career home run - while playing for which Major League team?
   a. Texas Rangers
   b. St. Louis Cardinals
   c. Atlanta Braves
   d. Boston Red Sox

2. Which country won their third FIFA World Cup title at the 1970 championship in Mexico?

    a. Brazil
    b. France
    c. Spain
    d. Uruguay

3. True or False? When the city of Sapporo hosted the 1972 Winter Olympic Games, it was the first time in history that the competition had been held in Japan.

4. When he won the PGA Championship in 1971, who became the first golfer in the sport's history to win two career grand slams, securing victory in all four major tournaments for the second time?

    a. Andy North
    b. Jack Nicklaus
    c. Johnny Miller
    d. Billy Casper

5. When they defeated the Washington Redskins to win Super Bowl VII in 1974, which team became the first (and to date, the only) team in NFL history to complete a perfect undefeated season?

    a. Oakland Raiders
    b. Miami Dolphins
    c. Green Bay Packers
    d. New England Patriots

6. In what year of this decade was Billie Jean King's famous Battle of the Sexes tennis match played against Bobby Riggs?

a. 1970
b. 1973
c. 1976
d. 1979

7. Which of these legendary boxing clashes saw Muhammad Ali regain his heavyweight world championship title in a knockout fight against George Foreman in 1974?

    a. The Thrilla in Manilla
    b. The Fight of the Century
    c. The Brawl in Montreal
    d. The Rumble in the Jungle

8. Which champion thoroughbred racehorse became the tenth winner of the American Triple Crown in 1977, and the first horse in American racing history to secure the title undefeated?

    a. Secretariat
    b. Seattle Slew
    c. American Pharaoh
    d. Affirmed

9. In what year did the Pittsburgh Steelers win Super Bowl XIII to become the first team in NFL history to win three Super Bowl titles?

    a. 1971
    b. 1974
    c. 1976
    d. 1979

10. After over 50 years, which tennis major was held at the West Side Tennis Club for the final time in 1977?

a. Wimbledon
b. French Open
c. Australian Open
d. US Open

ANSWERS

1. C. Atlanta Braves. Having broken Babe Ruth's record, Aaron went on to retire with a total of 755 home runs in 1976. He remained the MLB career leader for the next 33 years until his own total was surpassed by Barry Bonds in 2007.

2. A. Brazil. Brazil is the most successful national team in FIFA World Cup history: they had already been crowned the winner in 1958 and 1962, won for the third time in 1970, and would go on to win the title again in both 1994 and 2002.

3. True. Japan had already hosted the Summer Olympics, held in Tokyo in 1964, but the Sapporo Games were the country's first Winter Olympics (as well as the first held in Asia). Japan would go on to host the Winter Olympics a second time, at Nagano, in 1998.

4. B. Jack Nicklaus. Nicklaus' domination of the sport in the 1960s and 70s had already seen him become the youngest player to win all four golf majors in 1966, at the age of just 26. He went on to secure a third career grand slam title in 1978 when he won the British Open Championship for the third time.

5. B. Miami Dolphins. Led by coach Don Shula, the Dolphins not only achieved the only perfect season in NFL history but also took the league in both points scored and fewest points allowed - all

despite losing starting quarterback Bob Griese to a broken ankle in the season's fifth week!

6. B. 1973. Held at the Houston Astrodome in Texas, 29-year-old Billie Jean King won the game in three sets, 6-4, 6-3, 6-3.

7. D. The Rumble in the Jungle. Held in Kinshasa, Zaïre (the capital of the modern-day Democratic Republic of the Congo) on October 30, 1974, Ali won by a knockout in the eighth round. Despite going on to regain his world title, Ali was the 4–1 underdog in the fight, as Foreman was undefeated until then, and the undisputed heavyweight champion.

8. B. Seattle Slew. Only one other horse had repeated Seattle Slew's undefeated victory - his direct descendent, Justify, who won the Triple Crown in 2018.

9. D. 1979. The Steelers defeated the Dallas Cowboys by a score of 35–31 in Super Bowl XIII. Both teams were vying for their third Super Bowl title in the game, as they had earlier met in the NFL final of Super Bowl X in 1976 (which the Steelers also won, with a score of 21–17). Super Bowl XIII was ultimately the first rematch in NFL history.

10. D. US Open. The following year, the competition moved to Flushing Meadows.

DID YOU KNOW?

- One of the most famous sports plays in competitive history, the Immaculate Reception took place on December 23, 1972: with just 22 seconds of play remaining, the Pittsburgh Steelers star running back Franco Harris caught the ball as it bounced off the helmet of Oakland Raiders safety Jack Tatum to score a touchdown and secure victory for his side.

- The Philadelphia Flyers became the first post-1967 expansion NHL franchise to win the Stanley Cup on May 19, 1974.

- Olympic icon Bruce Jenner - now trans icon Caitlyn Jenner m- made history in 1976, when he (she) won the men's decathlon event at the 1976 Summer Olympics in Montreal, setting a third successive world record in the process!

- The first NASCAR Daytona 500 was televised live on February 18, 1979. Although it is seen as establishing the popularity of NASCAR racing in the United States, today it's better remembered for an infamous on-track punch-up between drivers Cale Yarborough and Donnie Allison!

- The 1976 Winter Olympics were infamously thrown into disarray during the voting process this decade, when the people of the original victorious host city - Denver, Colorado - voted in a referendum not to fund the event, forcing the city to turn the International Olympic Committee's offer down.

Things went from bad to worse when the IOC voters' second place city, Sion, in Switzerland, also turned down the IOC's offer to host the event - as did their third option, Whistler, in Canada. With time running out and still no host city chosen, the IOC eventually offered the games to the Austrian city of Innsbruck - which had already hosted the event just 12 years earlier in 1964!

BONUS ROUND

THE 1970s

1. What was the approximate population of the United States according to the 1970 census?
    a. 160 million
    b. 200 million
    c. 240 million
    d. 280 million
2. Three movies made more than $100 million at the global box office in 1978 for the first time. Which of these was NOT one of them?

a. The Deer Hunter

b. Superman

c. Grease

d. National Lampoon's Animal House

3. Which US state changed its flag in 1971, removing a pine tree from one side of the flag to leave an image of an Algonquin Native American on both sides?

a. Delaware

b. New Hampshire

c. Massachusetts

d. Oregon

4. What girl's name rose from the 20th most popular in the 1960s to the most popular overall in the 1970s in the United States?

a. Gloria

b. Julia

c. Jennifer

d. Lori

5. Which of these was the best-selling book in the United States according to *Publishers Weekly* in both 1972 and 1973?

a. The French Lieutenant's Woman

b. Jonathan Livingston Seagull

c. The Day of the Jackal

d. The Odessa File

6. And which of these classic children's novels was published in 1972?

a. Charlotte's Web

b. Watership Down

c. The Magic Faraway Tree

d. Matilda

7. The African republic of Guinea-Bissau declared independence in 1973 - from which European nation?

   a. Portugal

   b. France

   c. UK

   d. Spain

8. Which legendary jazz musician died in 1974 at the age of 75?

   a. Louis Armstrong

   b. Fats Waller

   c. Duke Ellington

   d. Charlie Parker

9. In what year of the 1970s was Jimmy Carter sworn in as the 39th President of the United States, did the space shuttle *Enterprise* go on its debut test flight, and did Queen Elizabeth II celebrate her silver jubilee?

   a. 1971

   b. 1974

   c. 1977

   d. 1979

10. Rising inflation in the 1970s caused the average price of a home in the United States to jump from around $27,000 at the start of the decade to what by the end of the decade?

a. $34,000
b. $43,000
c. $55,000
d. $74,000

ANSWERS

1. B. 200 million. The actual figure was 203,392,031, showing an increase of around one-eighth over the previous decade. Despite a rise of almost 25 million people since 1960, however, the US population increase was slowing and would continue to reduce toward the end of the century.

2. A. *The Deer Hunter*. Despite its acclaim and Academy Awards successes, *The Deer Hunter* grossed just under $49 million at the worldwide box office. *Grease*, meanwhile, ranked Number One in 1978, with a global gross of just shy of $160 million; *Superman* came in second with $134 million; and *National Lampoon's Animal House* defied expectations to make $120 million.

3. C. Massachusetts. Prior to 1971, the flag of Massachusetts was double-sided, with the Algonquin image on one side, and the pine tree on the other. The flag was simplified, although the pine tree - a longstanding symbol of New England - remains in use on the state's maritime ensign.

4. C. Jennifer. Over 580,000 babies born in the 1970s in America were named Jennifer, compared to just 164,000 in the previous decade.

5. B. *Jonathan Livingston Seagull*. First published in 1970, Richard Bach's classic allegorical novel had sold over one million copies by 1972 alone.

6. B. *Watership Down*. Richard Adams' debut novel was published in London in 1972, then in the United States in 1974 where it quickly became a best-seller; it ended the year as the second biggest selling title in the USA, after *Centennial* by James A Michener.

7. A. Portugal. Guinea-Bissau remains one of only a handful of countries in Africa where Portuguese is the official language, alongside the likes of Mozambique, Angola, and Equatorial Guinea.

8. C. Duke Ellington. Fats Waller died in 1943; Louis Armstrong died in 1971; and Charlie Parker died in 1955.

9. C. 1977.

10. D. $74,000. Nearly a three-fold increase, the actual average figure was roughly $74,200 in 1979, equivalent to over $310,000 today.

DID YOU KNOW?

- Showing the shift toward the modern world that took place in the 1970s, it was in this decade that the phrases *paternity leave* (1973), *politically incorrect* (1970), and *male chauvinist pig* (1970) were all first recorded in the language!

- The world's first email was sent in 1971 - and the @ sign was added to a recipient's address for the first time!

- The world's first cellphone call was made on April 3, 1973, by Motorola engineer Marty Cooper from the corner of Sixth Avenue in New York.

- History was made in Europe in the 1970s when Queen Margrethe II of Denmark became the country's first female monarch since 1412!

- The 1970s saw the arrival of several new and modern inventions, including the pocket calculator (in 1970), Post-It notes (in 1974), and the ring-pull push-through can top (in 1975).

PART 4:
THE 1980s

IN THE NEWS

THE 1980s

1. Ronald Reagan was sworn in as president on January 20, 1981. But what number president was he?

    a. 39th

    b. 40th

    c. 41st

    d. 42nd

2. The 1980s started off with some good news, when the World Health Organization officially declared that what disease had been eradicated, three years after the last known endemic case?

   a. Polio
   b. Smallpox
   c. Whooping cough
   d. Sleeping sickness

3. The 1980 eruption of Mount St. Helens affected an area of the United States far outside the volcano's home state of Washington. In total, the gigantic eruption deposited ash across how many US state's territories?

   a. Three
   b. Six
   c. Nine
   d. 11

4. True or False? Despite being known as the Falklands War, the UK and Argentina never formally declared war on one another in 1982.

5. Work began on the glass pyramid in the central court of the Louvre art gallery in Paris in 1981. Which world-renowned architect designed it?

   a. Norman Foster
   b. Frank Gehry
   c. IM Pei
   d. Jørn Utzon

6. In what year of the 1980s did Prince Charles marry Lady Diana Spencer?

a. 1981
b. 1984
c. 1986
d. 1989

7. In 1981, who became the first woman on the United States Supreme Court?

a. Ruth Bader Ginsburg
b. Sandra Day O'Connor
c. Sonia Sotomayor
d. Elena Kagan

8. What medical advance did scientist and inventor Robert K Jarvik pioneer in the early 1980s?

a. Kidney dialysis
b. Iron lung
c. Hearing aid
d. Artificial heart

9. Which unsuccessful 1980s presidential candidate nevertheless made history when he selected a female running mate and potential first-ever female vice president?

a. Michael Dukakis
b. Walter Mondale
c. George McGovern
d. Dan Quayle

10. In his landslide victory in the 1988 US election, George Bush became the first sitting vice president to be elected president for 152 years. Who was the last before him?

a. Martin Van Buren
b. Andrew Jackson
c. James K Polk
d. Zachary Taylor

ANSWERS

1. B. 40th. And Reagan's choice of vice president, George Bush, was America's 43rd holder of that title.

2. Smallpox. The last naturally occurring case of smallpox was recorded in Somalia in 1977, and the disease was declared eradicated in 1980. The disease remains the only human disease ever to have been eradicated to date.

3. D. 11. The disaster caused 57 fatalities, over $1 billion of damage (equivalent to triple that amount today) and killed tens of thousands of animals.

4. True. Despite its name, the ten-week conflict over ownership of the Falkland Islands (or Argentina's Las Malvinas) and the nearby archipelagic dependency of South Georgia and the South Sandwich Islands was never formally nor officially declared 'a war'.

5. C. IM Pei. Shanghai-born American architect IM Pei' audacious design of a vast modern-style glass pyramid was initially hugely controversial when work began on the structure in 1981, but it has since come to be as famous and as embraced as many of Paris' most famous landmarks.

6. A. 1981. The royal couple were wed on July 29, 1981, at St Paul's Cathedral in London. Incredibly, the lavish ceremony was watched by an estimated global television audience of 750 million people!

7. B. Sandra Day O'Connor. To date, out of over 100 justices to have served on the Supreme Court of the United States, only six have been female. Sandra Day O'Connor was the first, followed by Ruth Bader Ginsburg in 1993; Sonia Sotomayor in 2009; Elena Kagan in 2010; Amy Coney Barrett in 2020; and Ketanji Brown Jackson in 2022.

8. D. Artificial heart. The very Jarvik-7 artificial heart was implanted into a patient in 1982; he died 112 days later.

9. B. Walter Mondale. Mondale chose Geraldine Ferraro as his running mate in the 1984 election, which saw Ronald Reagan win his second term in office.

10. A. Martin Van Buren. Van Buren served just one term in office as the eighth president of the United States, from 1837 to 1841. In the 1836 election, the then vice president Van Buren secured an easy victory (50.8% share of the vote) over a divided pair of Whig opponents, William Henry Harrison (who won 36.6%) and Hugh L White (9.7%).

DID YOU KNOW?

- Space travel took a great leap forward in the 1980s, with the launch of the space shuttle *Columbia* on April 12, 1981.

- In the world of computers, on January 1, 1983, ARPAnet adopted TCP/IP protocols, allowing data exchange among a network of different models of computers. If that sounds confusing, then think of it this way: this great electronic step forward is seen as the birth of the modern world wide web!

- On June 19, 1983, Sally Ride became the first American woman in outer space when the space shuttle *Challenger* was launched.

- In an extraordinary and unexpected step forward in gender equality, on November 12, 1981, the Church of England voted to allow women to serve as priests for the first time.

- This decade also saw IBM release the world's first personal computer, the IBM Model 5150, on August 12, 1981. Unfortunately, it would be outclassed and outsold by the Commodore 64 personal computer the following year, which quickly became the highest-selling computer model of all time.

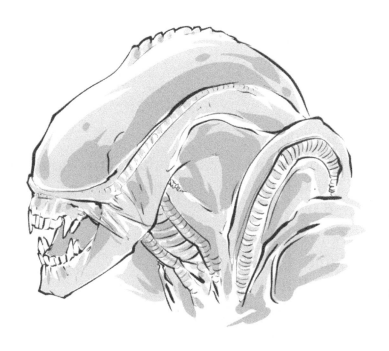

MOVIES & TV

THE 1980s

1. In what year of the 1980s was *The Oprah Winfrey Show* nationally syndicated for the first time?
   - a. 1980
   - b. 1983
   - c. 1986
   - d. 1989

2. And...True or False? *The Oprah Winfrey Show* received so many Daytime Emmy Awards that Winfrey herself chose to stop submitting the program for awards consideration.

a. What stage musical was adapted for cinema in 1982?
b. Fame
c. Grease
d. Annie
e. Hairspray

3. 1986 sci-fi horror *Aliens* was the follow-up to Ridley Scott's 1979 Oscar-nominated masterpiece. Who directed it?
   a. Stanley Kubrick
   b. James Cameron
   c. Tim Burton
   d. Steven Spielberg

4. For what 1982 movie did Meryl Streep receive her second Oscar and fourth Academy Award nomination?
   a. The French Lieutenant's Woman
   b. Out of Africa
   c. Ironweed
   d. Sophie's Choice

5. Who directed the 1988 Tom Hanks romantic comedy *Big*?
   a. Penny Marshall
   b. Rob Reiner
   c. Garry Marshall
   d. Cameron Crowe

6. Who was the villain opposite Michael Keaton's Batman in the 1989 comic book adaptation?

a. The Riddler
b. Catwoman
c. The Penguin
d. The Joker

7. And which musical legend contributed nine songs to the *Batman* soundtrack, releasing it as his 11th studio album in 1989?

a. Phil Collins
b. Elton John
c. Prince
d. Jon Bon Jovi

8. Sergio Leone's final film, *Once Upon a Time in America*, was released in a heavily edited form in the United States, with distributors cutting the film down to two hours and 19 minutes. How long had Leone's original cut of the movie been?

a. Two hours and 39 minutes
b. Two hours and 59 minutes
c. Three hours and 29 minutes
d. Three hours and 49 minutes

9. Which legendary English actor played the title character in the 1980 drama *The Elephant Man*?

a. John Gielgud
b. Anthony Hopkins
c. Ian McKellen
d. John Hurt

ANSWERS

1. C. 1986. An almost instant success, the show would go on to run for 25 seasons and more than 4,500 episodes before coming to an end in 2011; it remains the highest-rated daytime talk show in American television history.

2. True! In all, *The Oprah Winfrey Show* won 47 Daytime Emmy Awards until Winfrey stopped submitting it for consideration to give other shows a chance in 2000.

3. C. *Annie.* Written by Charles Strouse, Martin Charnin, and Thomas Meehan, *Annie* debuted on Broadway in 1977, and ran for a record-setting six years.

4. B. James Cameron. Despite going on to billion-dollar blockbusters and Oscar successes like *Titanic* and *Avatar*, James Cameron was relatively inexperienced when he was hired to write and direct the *Alien* sequel in the early 1980s. In fact, he had just two previous feature-length directing credits: 1984's *The Terminator*, and his B-movie debut, *Piranha II: The Spawning.*

5. D. *Sophie's Choice.* Streep was nominated for all four of those movies in the 1980s, having earned her first nomination for *The Deer Hunter* in 1978, and winning her first Oscar, for Best Actress in a Supporting Role, for *Kramer vs. Kramer* in 1979. In total, she was nominated for an Oscar six times in

the 1980s alone, won her third Oscar for *The Iron Lady* in 2012, and remains the most nominated performer in Academy Awards history.

6. A. Penny Marshall. A box office smash, *Big* became the first film directed by a woman to gross more than $100 million at the United States box office.

7. D. The Joker. The role was famously taken on by Jack Nicholson. Catwoman and The Penguin would appear opposite Keaton in the 1991 sequel, *Batman Returns*.

8. C. Prince. The first single from the album, "Batdance," was a Number One hit on the Billboard charts.

9. D. Three hours and 49 minutes. Leone's original 229-minute cut of *Once Upon a Time in America* remains one of his most acclaimed movies and is often cited as one of the greatest gangster movies of all time.

10. D. John Hurt. Hurt received the second of his career's two Oscar nominations and won the 1980 BAFTA Award for Best Actor for his performance.

DID YOU KNOW?

- Country star Dolly Parton made her big screen debut this decade *when 9 to 5* debuted in cinemas in 1980. It later emerged that she had only agreed to star in the movie - alongside Lily Tomlin and Jane Fonda - on the condition that she could write the theme song for it. She went on to be nominated for the Best Original Song Oscar at the 1981 Academy Awards.

- After 11 years and 256 episodes, the final edition of the sitcom *M*A*S*H*, "Goodbye, Farewell and Amen," was broadcast on CBS on February 28, 1983, and instantly became the most-watched television broadcast in American history with an audience of 105,970,000. It retained the title until 2010 and remains the most-watched finale of any television series. It is also the only one of the top 20 most-watched telecasts in the United States' history that *isn't* a Super Bowl!

- In 1980, a record 350 million people worldwide also tuned in to watch a memorable episode of *Dallas*, keen to find out who shot the character JR Ewing...

- The PG-13 movie rating was introduced in the 1980s when *Red Dawn* became the first movie ever to receive the rating. The rating was introduced following a raft of movies - including *Gremlins* and *Indiana Jones* - that were retrospectively deemed not graphic enough to be rated R, but not child-friendly enough for a standard PG!

- A classic movie character returned to the big screen in 1985, when Dorothy Gale reappeared in *Return to Oz*. Disney's movie production quickly hit a stumbling block though, when they discovered that the ruby slippers from the original 1939 were still under copyright at MGM. As a result, Disney was forced to pay an undisclosed licensing fee to allow the slippers to appear on screen once more.

MUSIC & POP CULTURE

THE 1980s

1. Michael Jackson's classic 1980s albums *Thriller* and *Bad* were famously produced by who?

    a. Prince
    b. Quincy Jones
    c. Rick Rubin
    d. Nile Rodgers

2. Which of these classic Andrew Lloyd Webber musicals debuted in 1984?

    a. Starlight Express
    b. Cats

    c. Jesus Christ Superstar

    d. Evita

3. Which of these musical technological advances made its debut in 1980?

    a. Minidisc

    b. Compact disc

    c. MP3 player

    d. Wireless headphones

4. MTV first began broadcasting in 1981. What was the first music video the channel ever showed?

    a. "Wuthering Heights"

    b. "Rio"

    c. "Video Killed the Radio Star"

    d. "Love Shack"

5. Which of these legendary pop acts scored more Billboard Number One hits in the 1980s than all the others?

    a. Stevie Wonder

    b. Whitney Houston

    c. Prince

    d. Lionel Richie

6. The 1985 *Live Aid* benefit fundraising concert was simultaneously held in which two US and European cities?

    a. New York and Paris

    b. San Francisco and Barcelona

    c. Philadelphia and London

    d. Miami and Edinburgh

7. …and which pop and rock star managed to perform in both Europe and America thanks to a supersonic transatlantic flight, ensuring make sure he made it to both venues on the same day?

    a. Freddie Mercury
    b. Elton John
    c. Rod Stewart
    d. Phil Collins

8. Which group had the first Billboard Number One of the 1980s with their hit single "Please Don't Go"?

    a. Blondie
    b. Pink Floyd
    c. The Police
    d. KC and the Sunshine Band

9. Jonathan, Jordan, Joey, Donnie, and Danny were the five members of what 1980s pop act?

    a. Boyz II Men
    b. New Kids on the Block
    c. Duran Duran
    d. New Edition

10. Which band's only Billboard Number One of the 1980s was entitled "Kokomo"?

    a. The Beach Boys
    b. Bon Jovi
    c. Cheap Trick
    d. Blondie

ANSWERS

1. B. Quincy Jones. Jones had earlier worked with Jackson on producing his 1979 hit album *Off the Wall* too.

2. A. *Starlight Express. Cats* had debuted three years earlier, in 1981; *Jesus Christ Superstar* in 1971; and *Evita* in 1978.

3. B. Compact disc. CDs first began to appear in record stores in 1980, and by the end of the decade had all but replaced earlier vinyl and phonographic records completely.

4. C. "Video Killed the Radio Star." The Buggles' classic 80s hit made history as MTV's first music video on August 1, 1981. It was followed up shortly afterward by "You Better Run" by Pat Benatar, and then Rod Stewart's classic hit "She Won't Dance With Me."

5. B. Whitney Houston. While Stevie Wonder and Prince both topped the charts four times in the 1980s, and Lionel Richie five times, in total Whitney Houston had seven Billboard chart-toppers this decade: "Saving All My Love for You" (1985), "How Will I Know" (1986), "Greatest Love of All" (1986), "I Wanna Dance with Somebody (Who Loves Me)" (1987), "Didn't We Almost Have It All" (1987), "So Emotional" (1988), and "Where Do Broken Hearts Go" (1988). Even more incredibly, all seven Number One singles were released consecutively, and

Houston remains the only singer in Billboard chart history to have had seven consecutive Number One hits.

6. C. Philadelphia and London.

7. D. Phil Collins. Held on July 13, 1985, the *Live Aid* concerts raised millions of dollars for famine relief in East Africa. Having performed at Wembley Stadium in London, Collins took a supersonic flight on Concorde to the United States, arriving (thanks both to the three-hour crossing time and the time difference) just in time to perform at the Philadelphia concert too!

8. D. KC and the Sunshine Band. The song was the band's fifth and last US Number One hit, following a string of chart-toppers - "Get Down Tonight," "That's the Way (I Like It)," "(Shake, Shake, Shake) Shake Your Booty," and "I'm Your Boogie Man" - in the 1970s.

9. B. New Kids on the Block. NYOTB was comprised of brothers Jonathan and Jordan Knight, Joey McIntyre, Donnie Wahlberg, and Danny Wood. Donnie's own brother, Mark (known professionally at the time as Marky Mark) was also an early member of the band when it formed in Massachusetts in 1984.

10. A. The Beach Boys. Incredibly, the 1988 smash hit "Kokomo" was the Beach Boys' first US Number One single since "Good Vibrations" back in 1966, 22 years earlier.

DID YOU KNOW?

- The 1980s were a good decade for gamers, with the arrival of *Pac-Man* in 1980, the Nintendo Entertainment System (or NES) in 1985, and the Nintendo Game Boy in 1989. When Nintendo released *Donkey Kong* in 1981, moreover, gamers met a character that was originally known as "Jump Man" - or, as we know him better today, Mario!

- The biggest hit of the 1980s in the United States was Olivia Newton-John's "Physical," which spent a record ten weeks at the top of the Billboard chart and sold two million copies. Oddly, though, Olivia Newton-John was not the songwriting team's first choice: before she recorded it, they offered the song to Rod Stewart and Tina Turner, both of whom turned it down!

- In 1983, Donna Summer made history, becoming the first female African American artist to have her music - the hit singles "She Works Hard for the Money" and "Unconditional Love" - on MTV.

- Michael Jackson's 1982 album *Thriller* sold 25 million copies in the 1980s alone - and has since gone on to sell 65 million copies in total, becoming the best-selling album of all time.

- The best-selling female-led album of the decade, meanwhile, was Madonna's third album, *True Blue*, released in 1986. She also had global successes with *Like a Virgin* in 1984, and *Like a Prayer* in 1989, and together all three titles helped Madonna become the best-selling female pop music artist of the decade.

SPORTS

THE 1980s

1. The 1980 Moscow Olympic Games were controversial because...what?
   a. No bronze medals were awarded
   b. Over 60 countries boycotted the event
   c. A new timing system was adopted for races
   d. No stadium announcements were made in English
2. Which Cincinnati Reds legend surpassed Ty Cobb's record of 4,191 career hits to become baseball's all-time hits leader in 1985?

a. Johnny Bench
b. Barry Larkin
c. Pete Rose
d. Joe Morgan

3. Which side memorably defeated the English cricket team on home turf in 1983, having never won a single match against England in 52 years of professional test cricket?

a. India
b. West Indies
c. Sri Lanka
d. New Zealand

4. In 1984, track and field star Uwe Hohn of East Germany scored over 100m in which of these events?

a. Javelin
b. Shot put
c. Hammer
d. Discus

5. History was made at Super Bowl XVIII when the Los Angeles Raiders defeated their opponents by a record-setting margin of 29 points, 38–9, in 1984. Who were they playing?

a. Kansas City Chiefs
b. Washington Redskins
c. Denver Broncos
d. Green Bay Packers

6. In 1989, who broke Gordie Howe's National Hockey League all-time scoring record?

a. Wayne Gretzky

b. Bobby Orr

c. Mario Lemieux

d. Steve Yzerman

7. Which team sport's World Cup tournament was launched in 1987?

a. Rugby

b. Soccer

c. Field hockey

d. Volleyball

8. True or False? Mike Tyson was just 20 years old when he became boxing Heavyweight Champion in 1986.

9. "Fernandomania" was a major upheaval in what sport in 1981?

a. Basketball

b. Ice hockey

c. Baseball

d. Horse racing

10. In which of the Grand Slam tennis tournaments did US tennis star John McEnroe famously lambaste the umpire with the memorable words "You cannot be serious!"?

a. French Open

b. Wimbledon

c. US Open

d. Australian Open

ANSWERS

1. B. Over 60 countries boycotted the event. In fact, no less than 66 nations - including the United States, West Germany, China, the Philippines, Argentina, and Norway - boycotted the Moscow Games entirely in protest over the ongoing Russian and Afghanistan War.

2.

3. C. Pete Rose. Rose would go on to end his career after 19 seasons with Cincinnati the following year, having scored a record 4,256 runs in total.

4. D. New Zealand. The New Zealand side had been touring England since 1931, with the somewhat lackluster track record of zero wins, 11 draws, and 16 losses from 27 games.

5. A. Javelin. No professional athlete before or since has ever thrown a javelin more than 100m, but Hohn's score was recorded as 104.8 m (343 ft 9¾ inches). In fact, the throw was so extraordinarily long that it came close to extending outside of the track and field area's central grass, and as a result, the IAAF was compelled to introduce a heavier and newly altered javelin design two years later that shortened legal throws. As a result, Hohn's record still stands to this day.

6. B. Washington Redskins. As well as setting a new record for the winner's margin of victory, the Raiders' score remains the most points scored by an

AFC team in a Super Bowl (although it was later matched by the Kansas City Chiefs in Super Bowl LVII, in 2023).

7. A. Wayne Gretzky. Having broken Howe's NHL all-time record with 1,850 points, Gretzky went on to score over 1,000 more and finished his career with an extraordinary 2,857 points to his name in 1999.

8. A. Rugby. Despite the sport's long history, incredibly, the inaugural Rugby Union World Cup was not held until 1987. Jointly hosted by Australia and New Zealand, New Zealand eventually secured victory over their fellow hosts 30–16 to take the first-ever world title.

9. True. In fact, Tyson was the youngest Heavyweight Champion in the sport's history.

10. C. Baseball. During the 1981 Major League Baseball season, the Los Angeles Dodgers took on 20-year-old Mexican rookie Fernando Valenzuela, sparking "Fernandomania" across the sport. Valenzuela's fiery playing style outfoxed many of his opponents, and he quickly led the majors with 180 strikeouts. For his efforts, he went on to be named Rookie of the Year and won the National League Cy Young Award.

11. B. Wimbledon. McEnroe's outburst came after one of his shots against his opponent, fellow US star Tom Gullikson, was called out. For his unsportsmanlike conduct, McEnroe was docked a point, but he went on to win the match all the same - and eventually took the title!

DID YOU KNOW?

- The San Francisco 49ers made history this decade, when they won four Super Bowl championships in 1981 (Super Bowl XVI), 1984 (XIX), 1988 (XXIII), and 1989 (XXIV). They then went on to win their fifth title in 1994!

- At the Seoul Olympics in 1988, Romanian gymnast Daniela Silivaş equaled fellow Romanian Nadia Comăneci's 1976 record of seven perfect tens in one Olympic Games. She went on to win three gold medals for her efforts.

- In 1982, the New York Islanders made history when they outplayed the Vancouver Canucks to become the first American NHL team to win three consecutive Stanley Cup titles.

- History was made in 1986 when cyclist Greg LeMond became the first American in the sport's history to win the prestigious Tour de France.

- In 1984, Los Angeles hosted the Olympic Games for the second time, having hosted it earlier in 1932. After the widespread boycotting of the 1980 Moscow Olympics, however, a bloc of over a dozen Eastern European nations - led by the Soviet Union - boycotted the 1984 Los Angeles Olympic Games in retaliation!

BONUS ROUND

THE 1980s

1. Which famous figure was awarded the 1984 Nobel Peace Prize?
    a. Mother Theresa
    b. Archbishop Desmond Tutu
    c. Henry Kissinger
    d. The Dalai Lama

2. True or False? The wreck of the doomed ocean liner the *Lusitania* was found on the Atlantic seabed in September 1985.

3. In what month was John Lennon shot and killed in New York in 1980?
    a. January
    b. March

c. August

d. December

4. The 1980 US census discovered that for the first time in history a state had amassed a population of over 20,000,000. Which state was it?

   a. Texas
   b. New York
   c. Pennsylvania
   d. California

5. The 1980 census also showed that what city had overtaken Detroit to become the United States' fifth largest?

   a. Phoenix
   b. Omaha
   c. San Francisco
   d. Houston

6. How much was one gallon of gasoline in the United States in 1980?

   a. $1.19
   b. $1.49
   c. $1.99
   d. $2.49

7. Which of these boy's names was NOT one of the three most popular in the United States in the 1980s?

   a. Matthew
   b. Michael
   c. Ryan
   d. Christopher

8. And for the first time, what was the most popular girl's name this decade in the United States?

    a. Amanda
    b. Jessica
    c. Patricia
    d. Melissa

9. The last time the average house cost less than $100,000 in the United States was 1986. What was the median house price that year?

    a. $62,000
    b. $72,000
    c. $82,000
    d. $92,000

10. In 1982, the US cent piece was changed from 95% copper to just 2.5% copper. What was the rest of the coin made from?

    a. Tin
    b. Zinc
    c. Iron
    d. Nickel

ANSWERS

1. B. Archbishop Desmond Tutu. A tricky question, as all four of those listed are Peace Price laureates: Mother Theresa was awarded the prize in 1979; Kissinger had earlier won it in 1973 (alongside his North Vietnamese negotiating partner Lê Đức Thọ); and the Dalai Lama was the recipient in 1989. Archbishop Tutu was awarded the 1984 award, however, officially in recognition of "his role as a unifying leader figure in the non-violent campaign to resolve the problem of apartheid in South Africa."

2. False. Actually, it was the wreck of the *Titanic* that was at long last located 13,000 feet down on the ocean floor on September 1, 1985, 73 years after it had sunk.

3. D. December. Lennon was shot four times by deranged fan Mark David Chapman at around 10.50 p.m. outside his apartment building in New York on December 8, 1980. He was pronounced dead just 25 minutes later. It eventually emerged that Chapman had waited outside the building that afternoon and at around five o'clock had asked Lennon to autograph a copy of his album *Double Fantasy* for him.

4. D. California. In fact, the population of California in 1980 was 23,667,902 — an increase of over 18% in the past ten years. The population of New York, actually, had fallen by almost 4% since 1970 and was now just over 17.5 million.

5. D. Houston. Houston had been ranked sixth in 1970 but rose to fifth with a population of 1,595,138 in 1980, outranking Detroit by almost 400,000 people.

6. A. $1.19. Though somewhat cheap by modern standards (though still equivalent to over $4 per gallon today), the 1980 price showed a marked increase on the previous year thanks to the instability of the recent Iran–Iraq War.

7. C. Ryan. Actually, Ryan was ranked 14th overall in the 1980s. Most popular of all was Michael (with 663,827 registered births from 1980 to 1989), followed by Christopher (with 554,909) and Matthew (with 459,019). Joshua, David, James, Daniel, Robert, John, and Joseph rounded out the Top Ten.

8. B. Jessica. The previous 1970s leader Jennifer (with 440,896 births) dropped down to second place in the 1980s, closely edged out by Jessica (with 469,518).

9. D. $92,000 (equivalent in modern terms to just over a quarter of a million dollars.) The following year, the average price had risen to $104,500, breeching the six-figure mark for the very first time.

10. B. Zinc. The penny was originally 100% pure copper when it was first minted in the 18th century but has been at least partly comprised of zinc (or a similar metal) since the 1850s. One-cent pieces minted after 1982 are now almost entirely made of zinc (97.5% by weight), coated in only a fine layer of copper.

DID YOU KNOW?

- The 1980s saw the arrival of disposable cameras, single-use contact lenses, and the portable CD player!

- The medical world achieved two great steps forward in the treatment of everyday conditions in the 1980s: having been invented in 1972, the antidepressant Prozac entered medicinal use in 1986 - the same year that nicotine patches were patented in the United States as an effective treatment in cigarette addiction.

- A series of protests took place in Burma (now Myanmar) in the summer of 1988, culminating on August 8 - which is why the event has since become known as the 8888 Uprising!

- Having thought up the product in the 1970s, McDonald's introduced the first Chicken McNuggets in its American stores in 1981, before the product was rolled out worldwide two years later.

- The 1980s had a slang all to its own. It was in this decade that the words *beer goggles* (1987), *yuppie* (1981), *sleazeball* (1981), and *cringey* were all first used (1986).

CONCLUSION

And with that final set of tricky questions and troublesome trips down memory lane, your *Baby Boomer Trivia Book* is complete! Four decades of history and headlines, political intrigue, and pop culture are now behind us. So how did you fare?

If you have made it this far, you've answered no less than 200 tricky trivia questions, covering everything from TV chat shows to rock 'n' roll stars, the wreck of the *Titanic*, state flags, and even the cost of gas!

Not to worry if you made a few missteps along the way, of course - nor if you had to resort to taking a peek at the answers (no one was looking while you did it, I am sure!). There were some fiendish questions thrown in the mix here, after all, but hopefully even if you did zig when you should have zagged with some of these multiple choices, you still picked up a little bonus knowledge or a new favorite fact along the way!

11979027R00085